Robert Dodge

Tristam Dodge and His Descendants in America

With historical and descriptive accounts of Block Island and Cow Neck, L. I.

Robert Dodge

Tristam Dodge and His Descendants in America
With historical and descriptive accounts of Block Island and Cow Neck, L. I.

ISBN/EAN: 9783337182786

Printed in Europe, USA, Canada, Australia, Japan

Cover: Foto ©ninafisch / pixelio.de

More available books at **www.hansebooks.com**

𝕿𝖗𝖎𝖘𝖙𝖗𝖆𝖒 𝕯𝖔𝖉𝖌𝖊

AND

HIS DESCENDANTS IN AMERICA

WITH HISTORICAL AND DESCRIPTIVE
ACCOUNTS OF BLOCK ISLAND AND COW NECK, L. I.
THEIR ORIGINAL SETTLEMENTS

BY

ROBERT DODGE

SUBSCRIPTION

NEW YORK
PRESS OF J. J. LITTLE & CO
1886

INTRODUCTION.

AT this long interval of over two centuries since
my ancestor came from England to the new world
of America, and in his age, when earnest men were
too much engrossed with the cares of existence to
pause for their own record of the immediate occasion of their movements, any more than the soldier
can halt, whilst the battle is in progress, to furnish
its history; when, even in our own day, of such
wide circulation for like objects, unless the traveler
become official or inscribed as member of some corporate or other permanent association, or prominent
in his new settlement:—it alike grows impossible
even in the lapse of ten years, or less, to trace their
existence or the causes of their emigration:—at
that epoch, so long before the era of the press,
telegraph, or post-office, when the geography of
the country was so little known beyond the few
northern sea-ports, the whole interior of the conti-
nent an unexplored wilderness, and, although the
excellent New England system of recording by the

Town Clerk each birth, marriage, and death in thei
towns, as well as grants of land and membership ii
their Church, where such membership was an indis
pensable condition for civic rights or the capacit)
to hold land ; never prevailed in the new settlemen
by Roger Williams and his fellow-exiles for freedon
of conscience on Narragansett Bay ; that gathere(
from the Old and New World all those who suffere(
from persecution, where no man was questioned fo
his opinions by any human authority ; and Rhod(
Island never had any such custom of record ; evei
that of deeds and wills was then and for man)
years unprovided, and no law for the record o
births, marriages, or deaths existing there befor(
1856 ; which even then was left of almost voluntar)
compliance, without adequate penalty :—it is caus(
for special gratitude, when pursuing this filial dut)
of research for the foot-prints of our ancestor, in th(
darkness of that early age, and the entire silence o
New England Town Records of himself or his fou
sons prior to the eighteenth century ; that the firs
and only record that we have is the careful, thoug]
incomplete and rude, entries of that venerabl(
chronicle—the ancient parchment volume, so long—
even to our day—the only record of Block Island
being the " Evidences of Property of the town o

New Shoreham, Rhode Island, otherwise called Block Island." They were contemporary, and much used ; by 1695 had become worn out ; when the present volume one, duly copied, as he certifies, from the earlier original, was prepared by faithful Nathaniel Mott, Town Clerk.

These few coeval entries and records furnish from that remote past the highest possible evidence ; so that, were any question to arise touching life or property, they would be accepted as absolute verity ; and yet they are incomplete, giving no home or lineage in England, place or date of birth, time or circumstances of arrival, or date of death. But his record as one of the sixteen purchasers and original settlers—in April, 1661—is carefully given, as well as of the meetings in Roxbury, Massachusetts, at the house of Dr. Alcock in 1660, in which he shared, leaving the conclusion almost certain that our ancestor and his family of four sons must have then recently come to New England, and that they neither joined the exclusive church in either colony, Salem, Boston, Lynn, or Plymonth, held office, nor received grants of land therein ; but, exiled by the persecutions of Church and State in England, they sought refuge in their own independent domain of Block Island, where they established a pure

democracy of true civil and religious liberty, con
tinuing until our day :—whose adhesion was naturall
secured by Roger Williams when, later, he obtaine
a charter for his infant colony of Rhode Islanc
Their Baptist faith and practice—unbroken eve
since—and by our own line this great denominatio
having been introduced in New York, whence it ha
spread so largely over the Union, induced a clo.
research into the Baptist history in England and th
United States (perhaps never before as fully wri
ten), as well as an extended study of the politica
causes of his emigration. We are able, by th
deeds of his sons and of his grandsons at Cow Nec
and New London, as well as from other public con
temporary events; records of town affairs and free
men; to fix approximately his death, his own ani
their probable ages; the names of the first genera
tion; the boundaries of the " Dodge Lands " on th
island; their emigration, and settlement of Nev
London and Cow Neck; and with comparative accu
racy trace them through that obscure past dow
to our own day; following, by patient study, th
story of their constant advance over this broa
land; ever foremost in the struggle with hardship
and the perils of the wilderness; in the Province o
New York and the Western frontier. Patriot sol

diers and officers of the Revolutionary army, though their wives and children were flying from the murderous raid of Indians and Tories; active in aiding the infant Government on the conclusion of peace; and at the front in command against the same British marauding enemy in 1812; and already, in 1804, upon the cession of Louisiana, first to begin the State history of Missouri. And then, after leading successfully, when all others failed, in the Black Hawk War: General Henry Dodge—alike lineal descendant--organized his Territory and State of beautiful Wisconsin; in which he was emulated by his son, the late Augustus C. Dodge; who was among the first to begin his grand State of Iowa. Many of the same lineage did true service for the sacred Union in the late Rebellion; many still adorn the line of the army, and have won deserved laurels; whilst many more of his sons have achieved lasting fame in civil life by professional, literary, and scientific attainments.

Succinctly and faithfully to narrate the simple facts, from public record, has all the charm of romance; and in such a work of filial honor and duty, I feel assured of the hearty co-operation of every member of our numerous and wide-spread family: remembering the words of Macaulay, that: "A people or family who take no pride in the noble achievements of their ancestors, will never achieve anything worthy to be remembered with pride by their descendants."

With many, in the family line, but two brief entries suffice—their advent—and their departure. To their kindred, this short record of their life is full of suggestive, tender memories.

While with many, the record of their life is filled with active work for their generation, and graced with large reward. By the kindred of both this first Family Memorial and History should be cherished as a most precious heritage.

Every effort has been made to secure completeness and accuracy in the Genealogies; but, in the daily hurry of our very active and moving family; whose old homes, records, and circles, so constantly are given up for new advance, and lapse into fading memories; it grows very difficult to secure original and complete Family Records.

It is proposed, in order to secure desired corrections; and also a fitting Memorial for preservation and use in our families; to issue a second edition, with appropriate Tables for the several generations; after the subscription for this first edition is complete.

Such a second edition will, of course, be at an increased cost; will require considerable time, care, and correspondence ; and can only be insured by an adequate subscription insuring the success of this first edition.

The author is conscious of many defects: inevitable to a first edition of an original, historical research: for all of which he deprecates censure : but, he scarcely thinks that, in sound judgment, he would be thought constrained to expand, by rhetoric comments, the varied and abundant material of this narrative of succinctly stated and digested facts: only to increase the volume and thereby depart from his aim of studied reserve and brevity.

TABLE OF CONTENTS.

INTRODUCTION.

Difficulty of the subject ; without record, save the rude coeval entries at Block Island ; his adhesion to tolerant Rhode Island with the other settlers, and early founding the Baptist Church—the only Church on the island—show them to have been a company of Baptist Dissenters from England: and a research for the causes of their emigration educed a new and original History of the Baptists in England and here, in their political and social relations, and their suffering under the Stuarts and Tudors.

From deeds and other records his life period and of his four sons approximately determined ; the lives of his descendants of like enterprise and much achievement ; first to found the States of Michigan, Iowa, Minnesota, Dakota and Wisconsin, and their care to maturity ; with constant public service since ; and a genealogy as nearly complete as could be obtained for this edition.

CHAPTER I.

Historic study of his Christian name ; his English origin ; first appearance in America, 1-4 ; arrival at Block Island, and of first Town Meeting, 1670 ; Freemen, 5 ; confessions ; early deeds of sons, 7-8 ; and date of his death, 9 ; result of revived systematic persecution of Dissenters in England, from era of Elizabeth, 10 ; their only refuge in Holland or America ; their numbers before 1640, and by 1688, 11 ; persecution for 150 years never retaliated by the Baptists when in power, 12 ; and his life period coincident with the struggle in England against the Stuarts, and the birth of the leading Protestant Sects ; contemporary with Cromwell, Mil-

COW NECK, LONG ISLAND.

TRISTRAM DODGE

AND HIS DESCENDANTS IN AMERICA.

CHAPTER I.

OUR ancestor from England owed his *first* or *Christian* name to that classic of the "Age of Chivalry," viz.: "Tristan" or "Tristram," "le Roi." Its alleged date is about A.D. 740, and before the time of Charlemagne; when this theme, long time sung by the troubadours, from their oral tradition, was first embodied in form as an *Epic*, reaching the widest and most enduring popularity; while the *name* of this hero-king, like those of Homer's Iliad, pervaded the middle and later ages with its lustre, down to Chaucer, whose "Sir Tristram" portrays the chivalric *"Bayard;"* and in our day, that careful mediæval student, Sir Walter Scott, presents him anew in his elaborate story of the middle ages— Quentin Durward.

Its poetic antiquity, remote as the Greek ballads and myths that were embodied in the Iliad, or the Gothic legends of the "Niebelungen Lied," was preserved in the melodious "chansons" of the careful rhythm and dialect of Languedoc by the wandering masters of the "gaie science." The *troubadours;* whose influence, as they moved, and sang through all those barbaric courts, castles, tournaments, and wherever knighthood or their ladies assembled, were the reforming element of that rude age, potent as the church, and to whom we owe the Latin tongues of Southern Europe, their advanced culture, and thereby the civilization of modern Europe.

It may now fall strangely on our prosaic ears; yet, to the students of the "Heroic Age," its traditions and verse are as enkindling as those of its associates; the legends of King Arthur, the Knights of his Round Table, Sir Launcelot, and the Holy Grail.

To *us*, it is of special interest, that so far down in the centuries, and through the darkness and tumult of English history, a thousand years after the alleged era of "Tristan," or "Tristram le Roi"; his name and renown should have become, through the Normans, so deeply rooted in rude Saxon England that it was cherished through every age, even during fierce Puritan zeal, to the restoration of the

Stuarts, and then was transported to our new world, where it is preserved in his lineage down to our own generation.*

"Sir Tristram" was a poetic creation as a history of the great knight of the *Lyonnais*, the name in romance for a part of Cornwall, England. He was an *English* knight and next to Sir Launcelot, or Galahad, the most renowned of the Knights of the Round Table. His *exploits*, as well as his *love of Yseult*, daughter of the King of Cornwall, and his

---

* "Encyclopedia Britannica," article, "Poetry." (Its European history.)

"The third class of Romantic traditions *then* (from about A.D. 740–814) first embodied in poetry, were those relative to the fabulous King Arthur, begirt with British and Armoric knights ; by far the most interesting of which is the celebrated legend of a pathetic or elegiac character, which bears the name of '*Tristan*' or '*Tristram*.' Among all the great epic poems of love and chivalry in the middle ages, says Frederick Schlegel, the first place is given by all nations to *Tristram;* but that we may not be fatigued with uniformity of fiction, the airy and lively legend of Launcelot is placed by the side of the more grave and elegiac representative."— *Webster.*

"'Tristram Sir,' the hero of an old Cymric romance, whose adventures form an episode in the incidents of Arthur's court, and are related by Thomas the Rhymer, as well as by many romancists. The original meaning of the name is said to have been '*noise*' and '*tumult*,' but from the influence of Latin upon Welch, it came to mean '*sad*.' In Europe, it regularly entered the ranks of the names of '*sorrow*.'"

aid to Arthur in driving the Saxons out of Wessex, *were all in England.* From the dawn of chivalry and the troubadours he had been the *Hero of Western England,* the theme of its bards, and the first ballad of its youth ; as the type of its *Heroic Age,* our ancestor's Christian name expressed and preserved its greatest memory.

Besides supplying to Ariosto much of his "Orlando," it has furnished many operas, as "Tristan le Roi" and "Tristan e Ysolde," by its Odyssey of love and adventure. The curious reader will find it amply told in Dunlap's History of Fiction, Vol. I., pp. 174–183, and in Tressau, Vol. IV., and it now re-appears as an English Idyll, by A. G. Swinburne.

Our ancestor appeared in America first in 1660 –1, as one of the original sixteen proprietors and settlers of *Block Island,* in the faithful official record of honest old Nathaniel Mott, town clerk, copied in 1695. The ancient scribe, though writing a strong legible hand, shows by his records of the old deeds that few or none of the Islanders of that age could write their names, and he expressed the several names by imitating their pronunciation ; and as with other settlers, our ancestor's name in his record "suffered a sea-change" by his pen, into "Thrustararorum Daudg," and "Thurstarorum

Daudge," Trustrome, etc., etc., until, long after those days, in the next generation, the influence of the school-master appears and rescues the name to its true orthography.

Of his origin : We may be sure he was not born in either of the New England settlements, as in all their careful records of births, and other records, his name does not appear.

Town Clerk Mott's detailed account of the preliminary meetings of 1660 shows that the settlers had then engaged and advanced the money to buy the island as their home for life. These serious acts could only have been executed by men who had at least reached their majority, or the age of twenty-one years.

He had been married sometime before : though his wife's name is not given, and in 1670, he had four sons with him as settlers, who were then admitted *freemen :* as appears [Book 1, Evidences of Property of New Shoreham (Rhode Island), page 55], viz. :

" At a Town meeting held the month of July for the year *one thousand six hundred and seventy :*

" It was resolved that the freemen of the Town their names should be recorded for the Town Record, "thyrustarom Daudge

" John Daudge

"thrustarum Daudge

" William Daudge

" Israel Daudge."

Thus, recording in 1670, nine years after he sailed, as freemen of the Town of New Shoreham or Block Island (though only in 1672 the Town was chartered by Rhode Island): first, our ancestor and then his four sons, viz. : *John, Tristram, William*, and *Israel Dodge*. He must have been married at least thirty years before, for his four sons to have attained majority and been admitted freemen in 1670. The father, then, on his emigration in 1661 must have been, at least, about forty years old, which would place his birth-year about 1620.

We have no record of the date of his death. His son and grandson bear the same name, and the several names are frequent on the records; the distinctions of Senior and Junior being usually omitted, it is difficult to determine which one was intended. But, at pages 90–3, "Confessions of Nathaniel Briggs and Trustram Dodge, Sen.," detailing verbatim allegations of the parties to a legal contest, then settled by the warden's advice, dated December 13, 1681, and 31st August, 1682, he was then living on the island perhaps at over sixty years old.

His name as "senior" does not again appear, but the name *Tristram Dodge*, without other designation, continues frequent in the records till 1735, which was after the death of his son and emigration of his grandson of same name to Cow Neck, L. I.

At pages 102 and 103 of Book 2, of the "*Evidences*," etc., we find a deed, dated 1st February, 172⅘, of release on voluntary actual partition, by William Dodg, and

Tristram Dodg, both of New Shoreham in the Colony of Rhode Island and Providence plantations in New England

and

John Dodg, of the Town and Colony aforesaid.

Reciting: that the parties did receive several tracts of land in New Shoreham which was their *father's :* Tristram Dodge lately deceased, who died intestate, and the said parties have ever since the death of their father held the aforesaid parcels of land in common. The one part of said land being near the middle of New Shoreham, by estimate 30 acres, bounded, etc. :

Second parcel on the East side of the Harbor (3

acres): Third parcel on the North side of the Harbor, "bounded South on the Neck fence, South-west on the pond, North and East on the Comon near the sea." (Reciting a survey, and locating each lot thereby) and Releases one Third. By their Deed of the same date, at p. 103,

John Dodg and

William Dodg: Release to Tristram Dodge several parcels of land at New Shoreham, left unto said parties by their father Tristram Dodge late deceased, "being known by the name of the Dodge Lands."

Both of these Deeds are signed by each son

his

by X

mark.

At page 40 *ibid*, we find the deed of

Israel Dodge   Date 1st October, 1720.

of New London Colony
Connecticut, late of Block
Island, to " My brothers "
John Dodge, Tristram Dodge, and
William Dodge of Block Island.

Conveying with full covenants, all his right, title, and interest in all the lands at New Shoreham, whereof his father Tristram Dodge had died seized, and intestate ; and the undivided share descended to him as one of the heirs in common.

There is no record of grant of letters of administration, and no other children or heirs are anywhere alleged.

That their father—the first settler—may have *died* in 1700–10, at 80–90 years of age, is consistent herewith.

After much research in England, we have been disappointed in our hope to be able to give from his English home the exact dates of his own birth and that of his four sons, and only children, who survived and emigrated ; and further knowledge of his wife, family, and their ancestral home.

On this record ; evidence of the highest character, it is manifest, that our ancestor and all his children were born abroad, and not in New England, before the arrival of William Dodge in the fleet settling at Salem in 1629 ; who was, probably, of his kindred; but of what, if any, affinity and in what year he came remains for further research, and we are even yet hopeful of some proof thereon: but he first appears in history in 1660 ; and may then have just arrived from England in Massachusetts, though only as a place of temporary sojourn, preparatory to permanent settlement on Block Island.

To gain a close view of the lives of our earliest ancestors, in an era when the humblest education was rare, so that none of the executive class, as we may call the great majority, were able or willing to record the facts, motives, or aims of their public conduct, we must resort to established history for the chief events controlling their daily lives, and frame our own conclusions therefrom.

By public records—statutes, and their enforcements—we know how the enthroned Church of England, from the era of Queen Elizabeth, by law begirt all Dissenters with systematic, constant, inquisitorial persecution; by heavy fines, confiscation, pillory, prison, exile, torture, and martyrdom.

With ever renewing devotion to their chosen tenets, successive generations suffered without revolt, but with unswerving loyalty to their royal oppressors and patriotism.

Their only refuge was exile to Holland; for centuries the sole nation in Europe of enlightened tolerance; but there the English refugees languished in hopeless and obscure poverty; or, last of all, banishment to what they thought the impenetrable and savage wilderness of far distant America; beyond the vast ocean, whose perils must be crossed, only to meet wild beasts and Indians fiercer still. Long did the Dissenters hesitate and suffer before venturing on the treacherous ocean for their last resort.

Prior to the memorable assembling of the Long Parliament, in 1640, the English Calvinists in the New World of America had reached to twenty thousand souls; with small resources: and so continued till 1660, when the restoration of the combined tyranny of Church and Crown reviving the sharpest rigors of the despotic Tudor law, drove into American exile increasing numbers that steadily grew, for many years, unchecked even by the promises of the Revolution of 1688.

Dissenters in religion from the English Church were mostly Republicans in political opinion, and their persecution was thought essential to the security of the State. Oppression swelled their numbers and strength, and in 1640, rising to the front as the majority of the House of Commons in that immortal Parliament, they began the grandest epoch of English history. Every shade of religious and political dissent and opinion was there, each clamorous for the mastery; even emulating their former oppressors until their new license was checked by the dignified tolerance of Cromwell, Milton, Hampden, Marvell, and others, as they in turn secured supreme power.

For one hundred and fifty years, with brief re-
spites, Dissenters had suffered. When, in turn, they
gained supremacy, some grasped the chance of persecuting their former followers in adversity.

Among those conflicting sects, in this chaos of
creeds, the Baptists held their own distinctive
tenets stoutly as the rest; but never with the
persecuting spirit of the ambitious Presbyterians,
whose laws surpass those of the reign of Elizabeth.

In 1660, escaping from the furnace of the revived
fires of persecution in England, our lineal ancestor
—Tristram Dodge—with his four sons, then grown
to manhood, first appear in the Colony of Massachusetts Bay, recent arrivals from England. Their
home of origin may yet be discovered. It was,
probably, Devonshire, or its vicinity, and allied to
the old Cheshire stock. His life-period, 1620—
1700-10 (James I. to Anne), was the tempestuous
era of struggle against the tyranny of church and
king, that brought forth the grand English Commonwealth, Cromwell, Milton, the execution of the
King in 1649; the revolting submission, shame, and
license of the Restoration; the bitter persecution of
James II.,—his exile; the Constitutional Revolution of 1688, and Queen Anne; with the develop-

ment of a Protestant Church, Puritans, Independents, Presbyterians, and Baptists.

If he left England about 1660, he could not fail to have witnessed or shared under the Lord General Cromwell, "*chief of men*," in the fierce struggle of the time; and probably in those days of bloody reaction, that swayed the English at the Restoration, when like Goffe, and many other sincere Puritans, he sought secure retreat beyond the seas, and found his fitting home on Block Island.

He had been contemporary with John Bunyan (1628–88), whose spirit seems to have directed his course and that of his descendants.

At the Restoration of 1660, the fierce revulsion of the Cavaliers, that shrank not from digging up the corpses of Cromwell, Ireton, and Bradshaw, subjecting them to mock trial with the old horrors of the sentence for treason, and then impaling their heads on Westminster Hall, was of such undisguised ferocity that the former triumphing Puritans were no longer seen or heard of in England. A large number affected extreme loyalty to lull suspicion, but many who had been active and earnest in the great Rebellion, if they would remain, were obliged, like Milton, to seek concealment; while great numbers fled to remote New England, beyond the seas.

and reach of the blood-thirsty mob that gained the smiles of the royal Stuart and his advisers by their brutal violence to all who adhered to the principles of the commonwealth or a free church.

Doubtless this tempest in Church and State, at the era of the Restoration, induced our ancestor to join in the New World, with his family of four sons, that very large colony already gathered in New England, which, according to the careful research of Prof. John Richard Greene (History of the English People, Vol. 3, Book 7, Chap. 6): "between the sailing of Winthrop's expedition, and the assembling of the Long Parliament (1629-40), in eleven years two hundred emigrant ships had crossed the Atlantic, and twenty thousand Englishmen found a refuge in the West. The two hundred who first sailed for Salem (1629), were soon followed by John Winthrop with eight hundred men, and seven hundred more soon followed. Nor were they broken men, as they were in great part men of the professional and middle classes, some of large landed estates, some zealous clergymen, like Cotton, Hooker, and Roger Williams. They were driven forth from their fatherland, not by earthly want, greed of gold, or love of adventure, but by the fear of God and zeal for a Godly worship."

If this were so at the milder era prior to 1640, how vastly must this emigration have increased under the subsequent Stuart tyranny and the fierce Saturnalia of the Tories at the Restoration, when the Non-conformist clergy were deprived and thrown into jail, or abject life-long poverty, and men's lives and liberties were no longer safe from violence. Doubtless he only yielded to mortal terror before his exile from the old land; that so shortly before, under the Commonwealth, had been the home of true liberty regulated by wise laws.

His life-period (1620–1700) is of such marked coincidence with those great epochs of English history, that in his day enlisted so many in England actively to take part for the King and tyranny, or the Parliament and Liberty; that it requires no imagination to outline the panorama in which he lived.

His emigration to America with all his family—four grown sons—and property, for the life-residence of himself and all his descendants about 1660; and the significant fact that he refused to cast his heritage with intolerant and exclusive Massachusetts Bay or Connecticut colonies; but joined his fortunes and theirs with those of Roger Williams and liberal Rhode Island, previously securing his practical in-

dependence by becoming one of the original owners
and settlers of Block Island; and further, that established by his grandchildren the only church on
Block Island, *now* and *always sustained* and officered
by his descendants, is *the Baptist Church;* when
duly considered, might warrant the conclusion,
that he *may* have been prominent for civil and religious liberty against the King and Cavaliers. But
merely military service, even so eminent as that of
the Ironsides of Cromwell, did not induce retalia-
tion at the Restoration.

"Quietly and without a struggle," says the his-
torian Greene, "as men who bowed to the inscrutable
will of God, the farmers and traders who had dashed
Rupert's chivalry to pieces on Naseby field; who
had scattered at Worcester the 'army of the aliens,'
and driven into helpless flight the Sovereign that
now came to enjoy his own again; who had renewed
beyond the sea the glories of Crecy and Agincourt;
had mastered the Parliament; had brought the King
to justice and the block; had given law to England,
and held even Cromwell in awe; *became farmers*
and *traders again*, and were known among their
fellow-men by no other sign than their greater sober-
ness and industry."

As a sect, the Baptists first gathered a church in England at London about A.D. 1614, or the middle of the reign of James I.; taking their origin by the small society organized at Amsterdam, that emigrated to London at that date.

"In the sixteenth century"—says Macaulay—"Quakerism was unknown in England, and there was not in the whole realm a single congregation of Independents or Baptists.".

Congregational in their church government, each society formed its own laws, and the exercise of private judgment was untrammeled. Denying all human authority, priesthood, or hierarchy, with infant baptism: insisting on Immersion as the only true ordinance for adult believers, who were equal before their Divine and only Teacher, Christ, in his Word—they embodied the best elements of Puritanism, without its intolerance, and have always been esteemed as cardinal exponents of true civil and religious freedom. They have always been a standing protest against Church Establishments and their perpetuity, by Episcopacy, or infant baptism; all human creeds, or any form of State control of conscience, so universal in Europe; whereby the Baptists, save only in tolerant Holland, were

2

prominently sought for and systematically persecuted by a long series of statutes enforcing the
Established Church.

"The Baptists," says Bancroft, "nurslings of
adversity, driven by persecution to find resources
within their own souls; when they came to found a
State in America, rested it on the Truth, that the
spirit and the mind are not subordinate to the tem-
poral power."

Their principles, so congenial to the spirit of the
colonists, with few exceptions, took early and deep
root; strengthened their successful resistance to
tyranny, and became a fundamental basis or Magna
Charta of the Constitution of the United States
and of each State.

From the feeble seedlings of Block Island they
have had a steady and immense growth, so that in
December, 1885, there were in the United States
three million five hundred and seven thousand and
seven hundred and three Baptists officially reported.

It is noteworthy and of special gratitude, that,
however persistently early legal constraint in New
England, Virginia, and Carolinas sought to found
Church establishments here, they all failed to take
root, and lapsed into oblivion; while the Baptist

principles became the cherished corner-stone of our national, civil, and religious independence.

" In England, during the civil war, the Baptists took active part," says Greene. " Lord Manchester suffered Cromwell to guide the army at his pleasure, but they were startled and alarmed by his dealings with these dissident recruits. He wanted good soldiers and good men, and if they were these, the Independent, the Baptist, the Leveller, found entry among his Ironsides. 'You would respect them, did you see them?'— he answered the panic-stricken Presbyterians, who always charged them with anabaptistery and revolutionary aims; they are no anabaptists, they are honest, sober Christians; they expect to be used as men." Theological speculation took an un-wonted boldness from the temper of the times. "Behold now this vast city," cried Milton, from London, " a city of refuge, the mansion-house of liberty, encompassed with God's protection. The shop of war there hath not more anvils and hammers working to fashion out the plates and instruments of armed justice in defence of beleaguered truth, than there be pens and heads there, sitting by their studious lamps, musing, searching, revolving new notions and ideas wherewith to present us, as with

their homage and fealty, the approaching reformation; others as fast reading, trying all things according to the force of reason and convincement."

The English Baptists as a sect were conspicuous
for loyalty and quiet obedience to the rulers of the
State and the powers that be; unlike the Presbyterians, who were bitterly intolerant and ambitious of supremacy over all classes in State and
Church; or the "Independents," "who," says
Froude, "were not meek like the *Baptists*, who
used no weapons to oppose what they disapproved,
but passive resistance."

The Presbyterian rancor in the act of 1648, im-
prisoning for declaring infant baptism unlawful, and
death to those who denied Christ or the Trinity,
was short-lived; and became obsolete on the early
ascendancy of the liberal spirit of Cromwell, after
the death of the King and the newly modelled Parliament had destroyed the Presbyterian ascendancy.
With all other acts of the Long Parliament at the
Restoration, this was treated as void, as being
passed during the King's enforced absence, or after
his death; while it was also held, that all laws of
previous parliaments and reigns, although repealed
by the Long Parliament, were, on the restora-

tion of the *King* to his throne, revived and in full force.

Under the Act 35th of Elizabeth (A.D. 1593) Non-conformists refusing to attend worship in the parish churches were to be imprisoned till they made their submission. Three months' time was allowed them to consider ; if at the end of that time they were still obstinate, they were to be banished the realm ; and, if they subsequently returned to England without permission of the crown, they were liable to execution as felons.

Thus, no sooner was Charles II. on the throne, viz., the 25th May, 1660—the date of his landing in triumph at Dover, preceded by his declaration of Breda, promising general pardon, oblivion of all political offences, and religious toleration, which, like the many official promises of his father, proved a snare to his subjects,—the frantic loyalists were suffered to pursue their defeated enemies to every extremity.

Yet, according to Froude, the better feelings of the magistrates and administrators of the law would have fain relieved its severity even in Bunyan's case, and allowed him to escape with a light penalty, if he had not by his conspicuous over-zeal forced them to his arrest and conviction. And even then, though detained in jail, which he illuminated with his divine dreams; he was supported there by his Bedford church, and allowed to attend its regular Sunday service in their chapel, where he and his Baptist brethren were tolerated during the whole twelve years of his nominal imprisonment, and until his release, May, 1672, by virtue of the Declaration of Indulgence of Charles II., repealing the severer Conventicle Act of 1670. And, in 1671, while lodging in jail, Bunyan was chosen their pastor, and preached regularly as such, and was allowed to receive the visits of all who desired.

It would seem almost certain that my ancestor adhered to the Baptist persuasion, from the constant prominence of his immediate family as Baptists in the church organization, that about the close of his life was established by them on Block Island; and from the significant fact that no other sect has ever been established there; and, also, that all the first settlers must have been singularly in unison with Baptist sentiments and principles, if not publicly professors of that faith.

CHAPTER II.

ALTHOUGH the holders of Baptist tenets in England were systematically persecuted from the era of the Reformation, Henry VIII., A.D. 1534, by his proclamations, inflicting banishment and death, and by royal commission to Ridley and Gardner of Edward VI., and martyrdom of Joan of Kent and others, they increased in numbers; and for their simple faith were martyred under Mary and especially persecuted under Elizabeth, by proclamation 1560, like that of her father, and by her Acts of Uniformity. They were hunted to the death, fined, whipped, and imprisoned for their religious convictions, like the early Christians. This was continued under James I., by whom in 1612 Edward Wightman, for denying infant baptism, was burned at the stake; followed by the High Commission Court of Charles I., where Laud wreaked his malice on all Dissenters and especially on the Baptists; who, however, like the faithful in the Catacombs of Rome, steadily grew in numbers and power, so that when this century of fruitless coercion and barbarity terminated, and a new era of hope dawned with the Long Parliament, they had, in 1646, forty-six churches in England; seven established in London, of which the first, in Devonshire Court, remains to our day ; and enjoyed religious liberty during the Commonwealth ; until the Restoration of 1660 found considerable Baptist churches in thirty English counties, six leading towns in Ireland, and very numerous in Wales. Persecution of unexampled rigor commenced immediately on the Restoration.

Throughout all this period of persecution, the Baptists had held their meetings for worship, often at midnight, in woods or unfrequented places, without announcement, or, if in houses, in unsuspected dwellings. The minister, disguised as a carter, with smock, high boots and whip, or as a laborer, being admitted through the roof, which was also the common escape of the assembly. No music or singing was permitted, and watchful sentries were placed to notify the approach of the enemy : viz., either the informer, vicar, or summoner from the High Commission Court.

"They have been taken from their peaceful habitations," says John Stoughton, "and thrust into prison, in almost all counties in England, and many are still detained in crowded cells, poor men, with dependent, starving families."

In 1660, John James was martyred.

In 1662, the Act of Uniformity was re-enacted and enforced.   Two thousand clergymen, including Baxter, Flavel, and about thirty Baptist ministers, with many others, were imprisoned, fined, or exiled for Non-conformity.   This was followed by the Act against Conventicles of 1664, the Five Mile Act, 1665, and the new Fine and Penalties Act of 1670.

"It was made a crime," says Macaulay, "to attend dissenting places of worship; a single justice of the peace might convict, without a jury; and for the third offence, sentence to transportation for years.   With refined cruelty, it was provided that he should not be transported to New England, where he would find sympathizing friends; and for return before the term of his sentence, he was liable to capital punishment."

On July 26, 1660, the Baptist churches of Lincolnshire, in their petition to Charles II., say:

"We have been much abused as we pass in the streets, and as we sit in our houses, being threatened

to be hanged if but heard praying to our Lord, in
our own families, and disturbed in our so waiting
upon Him by continual beating at our doors and
sounding of horns; stoned when going to our meetings; taken as evil-doers, and imprisoned when
peaceably met together to worship the Most High
in the use of his most precious ordinances. They
have indicted lately many of us at the sessions, and
intend to impose on us a penalty of £20—for not
coming to hear such men as they provide us."

The king replied only with fair promises, and the
persecution increased.

By November, 1660, Bunyan was imprisoned, followed in the next year by many other Baptist ministers.

The warfare upon Dissenters continued till the
Revolution of 1688, when persecution ceased; though
the Test and Subscription Acts, requiring all who
bore office, either public or corporate, to swear to
their faith in the Creed, and subscribe the Articles
of the Established Church, were enforced till their
modification by the Act of 1779; and even now the
same exclusive spirit rules in their Parliament.

Lord Macaulay says of the Toleration Act of
1689, "that its provisions were cumbrous, puerile,

inconsistent with each other and with the true
theory of religious liberty. All that can be said
in their defence is this: that they removed a vast
mass of evil without shocking a vast mass of preju-
dice. That they put an end at once and forever,
without one division in either house of Parliament,
without one riot in the streets, with scarcely a mur-
mur from the classes most deeply tainted with bigotry, to a persecution which had raged during four
generations, which had broken innumerable hearts,
which had made innumerable families desolate, which
had filled the prisons with some of whom the world
was not worthy, which had driven thousands of
those honest, diligent, and God-fearing yeomen and
artisans, who were the true strength of the nation,
to seek a refuge beyond the ocean, among the wig-
wams of red Indians and the lairs of panthers."

It seems strange to an American that it should
require near three centuries for the English nation,
whose historic boast is their common law of constitutional liberty, to acquire the elementary principles of true civil and religious freedom.

During this persistent warfare on their rights in
England, Massachusetts colony, sharing the same
pretensions of exclusive theocracy, was not back-

ward in imitation. Besides her shameless persecutions for suspicion of witchcraft, and of the Quakers,
and her banishment, in 1635, of Roger Williams for
his doctrines of religious freedom; she followed
these by a general ordinance, in 1644, of banishment and perpetual exile, with fines and imprisonment at discretion of the magistrate, against all who
held the Baptist tenets as to infant baptism and
religious independence.

From this condensed history, it is plain that my
ancestor, and all who like him sympathized with
Roger Williams, had no home in England or Massachusetts, and that he sought his only true abiding-
place—Block Island—which he placed under the
sheltering wing of what was then the only free
(chartered) colony of England—Rhode Island.

Without further pursuing our inquiry for the occasion of his emigration, while in that age, so deprived of the press or any record save the public
acts of monarchs or statesmen of eminence, that
with a private subject, we are left wholly to pre-
sumptions, we quote again from Greene :

"The sudden outbreak and violence of the persecutions (that arose on the Restoration), breaking up
of conventicles, the imprisonment of worshippers,

etc., turned the disappointment of the Presbyterians
into despair.   Many were for retiring to Holland,
others proposed a general flight to New England
and the American colonies.   Among the Baptists
and Independents there was vague talk of an appeal to arms."

By this episode-sketch of the tumult and persecution that pervaded Church and State in the England of our ancestor, from his birth about 1620 till
he and his four sons appear, in 1660–61, as settlers
of Block Island, sailing thither with his (fourteen)
associates from Massachusetts :—

I have rather sought to develop to my own clear
apprehension, and thereby portray the elements of
his character, than to invent his history, by the easy
process of imagining our resolute ancestor in eminent position of active zeal for the Commonwealth,
or defence of the persecuted Baptists.

He was manifestly not in favor or sympathy with
the Crown or its restoration.   His career in the
New World plainly indicates that he adhered to the
faith and practice of Roger Williams and the tolerant Baptists.   Yet, however earnest his convictions
in that tempest, he may have emulated the meek-
ness and moderation of many other Baptists, or

the studious quiet of Isaac Walton (1591–1683);
Thomas Hobbs (1559–1679), or his adversary Cud-
worth (1617–88), and others, whose opinions were
not aggressive, and who remained out of the strife
in word and action.

The armies were composed only of volunteers;
small in number, and never reaching over one-thir-
tieth of the population; so that the great majority
were not in the ranks, and but a very few in civil
office; and thus, in spite of revolutions, the ordinary
pursuits and trades went along in their old way. At
that period of English history, when most of the
nation could not read or write; without the newspaper and all modern means of intelligent opinion;
without proper highways or the steam engine, in a
small nation of about three millions, scattered over
a territory only one-third larger than the State of
New Jersey, but whose largest area was covered
with impassable forests and morass,—the rapidly
crowding events that make the history of that time
so interesting, even at this interval, could only have
been known on their date by a very limited circle of
the metropolis, and imperfectly and slowly reached
the mass of the people.

The nation was poor; nearly one-fourth of the
population were dependent on parochial relief as

paupers.   The average earnings of good mechanics was, according to Macaulay's careful research, not over 4s. 6d., or about one dollar a week; and the food of all below the very wealthy was only oatmeal, rye, and barley, without meat; whilst the army of the Commonwealth secured its choice recruits by the pay of seven shillings a week, an advance of nearly one-half their possible earnings.

If to this actual hardship be added the fact that all hope of social elevation was impossible, even in peaceful times, their despair would have driven large numbers to bleak and distant America for an independence.

It is not a little strange that Great Britain never had a census taken by law till 1801, while twice before, viz, in 1753 and in 1800, the bill therefor had been defeated.   It was at length adopted in imitation of the United States, but it has no such aims as securing a just taxation or apportionment of representation, and is made as an accurate basis for political and economic questions.

Beyond the army lines the kingdom preserved its old tranquillity; the Dissenting chapels, in dark corners of towns and cities, were the arenas of harangue on the new doctrines of Church and State, by all manner of untutored declaimers—Fifth

Monarchy Men, Ranters, Independents, Presbyterians, etc., etc.—each, in their uncouth way, attacking the Established Church and all other sects, with
equally strange and clashing theories of civil government. The great majority had no means of obtain-
ing correct and adequate knowledge of events or
sound opinions thereon.

Transporting ourselves, in thought, to the England of 1660, as our native land for all past generations, where our home was the imagined centre of
every comfort and domestic bliss; and in contrast
sterile, bleak, rock-bound New England, at immeas-
urable distance over the tempest-tossed Atlantic,
the Siberia of that age, to be voluntarily chosen as
our life-long home; quitting our native land forever, taking all our family and property: such a
resolution evinced the utmost courage and sacrifice,
only to be accounted for by persecution that rendered the much-loved home in England intolerable.

The irresistible attraction of his contemporary
history, in what seems now the grandest crisis of
England, must apologize for the extent of our
digression.

CHAPTER III.

LET us resume our narrative—with the adventurous party of fifteen settlers on board the *Shallop*, sailing from Taunton for "Block Island," April, 1661. Their voyage, of perhaps a day, brought Tristram Dodge with his four sons, and all his worldly goods, to their landing (by tradition) at *Cow Cove*, on the eastern shore, north of the present harbor, and but a short distance south of Sandy Point, the site of the present North-eastern Light-house ; and he, with the other settlers, entered the dense forests which then covered the island hills, peopled only by the savages in overwhelming numbers, without any protection ; and took possession of their allotments of all the lands of the Indians, by virtue of paper titles in Massachusetts ; to which the natives were strangers : and yet our entire history will be vainly searched for a similar example of uniform, unbroken, peaceful acquiescence by the aborigines. No history survives to tell how this was accomplished. The small company of white settlers must have conciliated their

3

vastly more powerful native neighbors by deeds
of charity, which were afterwards emulated by William Penn's colony of 1685.

The allotment of land, known for generations as
the "Dodges' Lands," was mapped by surveyors ;
but their map is no longer extant on the island,
and we find it described, at the time of the voluntary
partition after his death, between his four sons, by
their releases of 1720–3.

It extended across the island, from east to west,
through the "centre,' from the old harbor on the
eastern shore north of the present breakwater.

He was scarcely planted on Block Island, when
he bought of the Province of New York (1665) (by
the N. Y. Records—his license dated April 14, 1665)
the island of 500 acres, yet called "No Man's Land,"
lying two leagues south-west from Martha's Vineyard.

Of his four sons—Israel, John, William, and Tristram, Jr.—Israel is on record as purchaser and settler of land in 1694, in the North Parish of New
London, Conn. (now Montville), where he died in
1745.

The other sons and children, viz., *John*, *Tristram,
Jr.*, and *William Dodge*, remained on the island,
and became progenitors of a very numerous race ;
some of whom emigrated in after generations, and

whose descendants are now to be found in almost every State, and frequently in eminent stations.

The ancient records of New Shoreham occasionally contain entries of births and deaths, as well as of deeds and wills, which in Rhode Island was not by law required until 1856.

At page 44 of Book 1, Evidences, etc., we find, "an account of some persons born, marryed, and dyed on Shoreham."

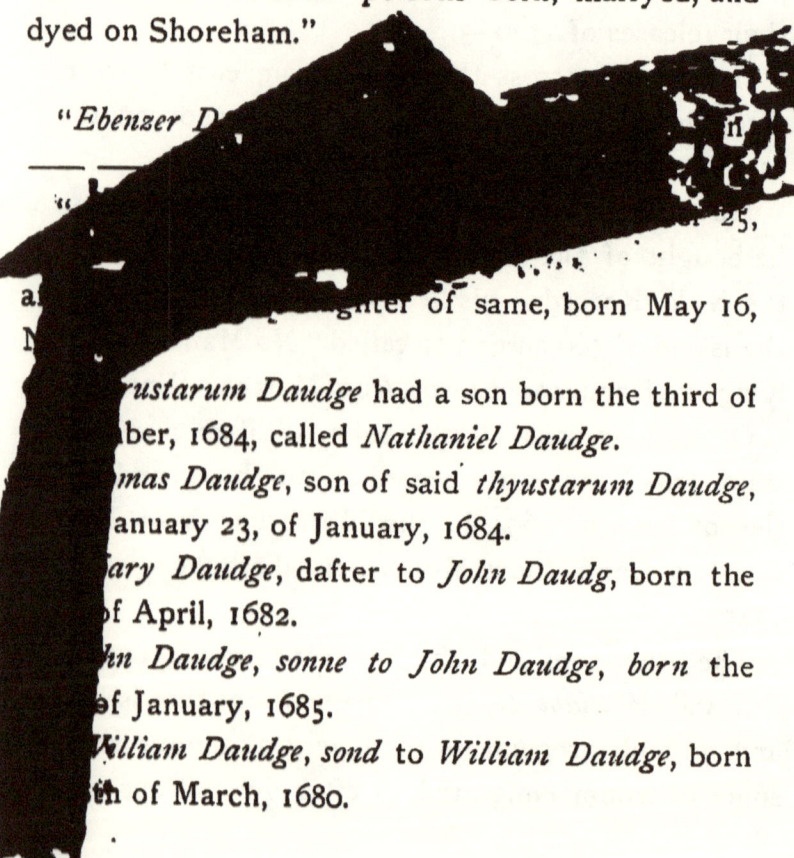

"*Ebenzer D*

ter of same, born May 16,

ustarum Daudge had a son born the third of ber, 1684, called *Nathaniel Daudge.*

mas Daudge, son of said *thyustarum Daudge*, anuary 23, of January, 1684.

ary Daudge, dafter to *John Daudg*, born the f April, 1682.

n Daudge, sonne to John Daudge, born the f January, 1685.

illiam Daudge, sond to William Daudge, born th of March, 1680.

" *Elizabeth, daftcr* to *William Daudge*, born the last of May, 1683."

———

And at page 89 and 97, *Ibid*, in the " Record of the Persones born and buryed in New Shoreham to 1683."

" *Nathaniel Dodge, son of Tristram Dodge, Senior,* born the second of November, 1681.

" *Mary Dodge, daught… of John Dodge,* buryed January …th 1683.

… …dg, Sr., born in Sep…

… …E…

23d of …

Jemara, born the 22d of S…   14, …

And in the   s La…

" Account of the persons born, married, an…

on Block Island in the year 1682,"   …d T

" *John Daudg*, Junior, son of *John Daudg*, …d …

died April the 16th.   N…

" *Mary Dodg, daughter of John Dodg, born* …d …
18*th*.

———

The above completes all the ancient coeval
of births and deaths of the Island Dodges. …
are necessarily the only evidence of origin,

inserted them in full, in their antique form. I annex another original of importance, being the Will of Tristram Dodge (2d). The same person is called "Senior" in foregoing record of persons born, etc., to 1683.

The Will following is invaluable, as supplying the only. Record of his descendants down to 1735.

Liber 2, Evidences, etc., page 211. Will of Tristram Dodge. Dated 26th day July, 1733.

"*First :*—Gives and devises to Dorcas my wife my house and all my land on Block Island for her life, and all my movable estate indoors and out ; and after her decease, the House and Land to my son Nathaniell Dodge ; and the movable estate to be equally divided between my two daughters Dorcas Landworth and Sarah Mitchell ; and my Will is that my son Nathaniell Dodge (who is named Executor) shall pay to my son Thomas Dodge Ten pounds ; and to my son Ebenezer, £10 ; and to my son Hezekiah, £10 ; and to my son Tristram Dodge, £10 ; and to my daughter Dorcas, £2 ; and to my daughter Sarah, £2." Revokes all prior wills (attestation clauses). Proved at New Shoreham, June 7, 1735.

These entries together show, as to the births and deaths, some uncertainty and carelessness, ex. g., children of *John Dodge* (Sen'r).

His *son—John* (at p. 44) is recorded as born 10 January, 1685, and at page 97,.Lb.,

" John," his son, died April the 16th, 1682, without stating—if such were the fact—that the former was a *second* son of like name; while Mary—his daughter's birth is given the same on both "records" as Ap. 18, 1682.

Nathaniel's birth-year is given in 1681 and 1684, 3d and 2d of November, in two entries by different clerks.

———

RECAPITULATION.

Their wives are not named.

John Dodge.　　　Children.

> *John (Jr.) born* 10 *June*, 1685.
> Mary　　　"　18 April, 1682.
> 　　　　　died 4 Jan. 1683.
> John (2d)　"　10 April, "

———

Tristram Dodge (2).　　Children.

Nathaniel, born 2d Nov. 1681 (or 3d Nov. 1684).

(1) Thomas,　　"　23 Jan. 1684.

Ebenezer, born 4 Oct. 1687.

Hezekiah, " *date not given.*

(2) Tristram (3), " " "

Dorcas, born May 16, 1694.

Sarah, " not stated.

*Josiah,** " 25 Dec. 1690.

———

William Dodge. Children.

William, born 8 March, 1680.

(3) Samuel, " 19th September, 1691.

Elizabeth, " "last of May," 1683.

———

Of the foregoing grandchildren,

1 *Thomas*   ⎫ Emigrated to Cow Neck (Long
2 *Tristram* and ⎬ Island), where they settled.
3 *Samuel*   ⎭ From Samuel descended a

large family of the State and city of New York.

From the remaining grandchildren descend the families on Block Island, which now are those of

Samuel Dodge,	John R. Dodge,
Edwin B. Dodge,	Noah Dodge,
Aaron W. Dodge,	Joshua Dodge,

———

* Is not named in will, and may have been deceased without issue at the time of the father's death.

Nathan C. Dodge,   William H. Dodge,
Solomon Dodge,   Uriah B. Dodge,
Amhad Dodge,   Robert E. D. Dodge,
Edmond Dodge,   W. Ray Dodge,
Welcome Dodge,   William M. Dodge,
Caleb W. Dodge,   Edwin A. Dodge,
James M. Dodge,   Burton B. Dodge,
Andrew J. Dodge,   Welcome Dodge, Jr.,
Richard A. Dodge,   Samuel A. Dodge,
John W. Dodge,   Ralph E. Dodge,
William Dodge,   Rainsford A. Dodge,
Lorenzo Dodge,   Simon Dodge,
Samuel P. Dodge,   Hiram Dodge,
James A. Dodge,   Gideon Dodge,
Samuel B. Dodge,   Leander Dodge,
Darias B. Dodge,   Edward Dodge,
John C. Dodge,   Nathaniel Dodge,
Joshua T. Dodge,   Edward T. Dodge.
Robert C. Dodge,

The foregoing list of family representatives is in-complete and with some inaccuracies, due to the failure to respond to repeated inquiries for the entire list and their respective descents.

The several families of Cow Neck are, viz. :

Tristram Dodge (3) of New Shoreham) : Grand-

son of settler of Block I. of same name. Married
November 28, 1741: Phebe (widow Adam) Mott.
Children: Joseph Dodge, who married Sarah Hicks,
July 28, 1763. Children:

Fanny, died 1843, single.

Penelope, married Schuyler Baxter, born 17 May,
1767.

Margaret C., died single, 1806.

Tristram Dodge (4), married Phebe Downing,
died, no issue, 1816.

William, born May 1, 1774, married Susan Hawley.

Charity married Isaac Downing, died 1815.

Joseph Dodge, Jr., married Cath. Cheeseman
(1816).

Isaac H., married Jane Burtis, 1805.

Sarah C., born 1788, died single.

Joseph Dodge, Jr. (died 1835) and Cath. Cheeseman.

Children: Hampton married 1st Sarah Underhill.

Married 2d, December 27, 1855, widow (Murrell).

Cheeseman married Martha Cornell, September
1, 1863.

Both reside in Buffalo, N. Y.

Isaac H. Dodge (died at Cow Neck, September
19, 1877) married

1808, April 20, Jane Burtis.

Children:

Martha B., married Henry Tredwell.

Sarah C., born 1816.

Joseph, born 1821.

Thomas Dodge (1), *son of Tristram* (2), born at
New Shoreham June 23, 1684, (about)
1712 married at Cow Neck, L. I.,
Susannah Hutchings.

Children—born at Cow Neck,

William—born May 15, 1714.

Mary   "   March 8, 1716.

Married Thos. Thorne, December 12,
1738.

Amos—born September 2, 1719.

Thomas (Jr.), born January 17, 1722,
died May 12, 1789.

Thomas Dodge, *Senior*, died at Cow Neck Homestead, where his tomb-stone is now in door-yard,
July 14, 1755.

His wife Susannah died April 11, 1778.

———

Thomas Dodge (2), *Junior*, in 1749 married Sarah
Onderdonk.

Children—born at Cow Neck,

Marie— " 1751, died do. December 15, 1831.

Peter, born 1753, died November 30, 1776.

Thomas (3), born June 15, 1755, died May 30, 1840.

Andries, born 1757, died October 28, 1762.

William, " October 16, 1761, died December 3, 1844.

Sarah, born 1764, died January 27, 1784.

William Dodge, born 1761, married Phebe Craft, died December 3, 1844.

Children :

Sarah Dodge, born September 19, 1789, died June 17, 1811, married J. Davis.

Martha Dodge, born June 9, 1791, died June 26, 1847, married Wm. Remsen.

Thomas Dodge (4), born July 2, 1793, died October 20, 1830.

Robert Dodge, born October 17, 1795, died December 10, 1857.

Peter Dodge, born April 13, 1798, died September 3, 1871.

Maria Dodge, born December 29, 1803, married W. Remsen—and widow.

Henry O., born October 13, 1805.

Peter Dodge (first) married Rebecca Ketchum.

Children :

Edward Dodge.

George K. Dodge.

Thomas Dodge.

Peter Dodge (second) married Hannah Ketchum.
Children :

William H. Dodge.

Alonzo P. Dodge.

Rebecca Dodge.

Thomas R. Dodge.

Thomas Dodge (3), married Elizabeth Monfort,
no issue.

Robert Dodge, married Susan Dodge (1795), son,
Isaac Dodge.

Henry Onderdonk Dodge, married (1st) Elizabeth
Craft, son, Jordan C. Dodge, born November
8, 1839; married (2d) Julia Oakley, children,
Miles W. Dodge. Henry T. Dodge.

Jordan C. Dodge (of Glen Cove, Long Island),
married Clara E. Kirby (1863), son, Herbert
A. Dodge.

Miles W. Dodge (of Philadelphia), married Nettie
F. Snedeker (1871), child, Ella I. Dodge.

Henry T. Dodge (Port Washington, Long Island).
Tristram Dodge, settled at Oyster Bay, Long
Island, where he died, 1763. Married Sarah
Hawxhurst, of Oyster Bay, at St. George's
Church, Hempstead, Jan. 13, 1726, children,

Stephen Dodge, who, 1783, settled in Nova Scotia,
pursuant to conditions of Treaty of Peace.

Daniel, who remained in New York.

Freelove, daughter, married Townsend Parish.
Among the signers to the Loyal Address of
Welcome, dated 20th October, 1776, to Lord
Richard Howe and General William Howe,
on their arrival at New York as Crown
Commissioners to the Colonies of "His
Majesty's loyal and well-affected Freeholders
and inhabitants of Queens County, on Nassau
Island, in the Province of New York, that
they 'bear true' allegiance, &c.," are:

" Tristram Dodge,"

" Daniel Dodge,"

" Ezekiel Roe and others."

This testator was a descendant of the " early
settlers of Cow Bay." As appears by his will,
his only sons were Daniel, who remained in
New York, and Stephen, who, in 1783, with
his family, emigrated to Nova Scotia; his
daughters, Sarah and Anne, died single, and
Freelove married Townsend Parish. Of his
son Daniel, his son Daniel, Jr., died without
issue in New York city about 1814, and this
branch is believed extinct.

CHAPTER IV.

STEPHEN DODGE was the son of Tristram Dodge, of Oyster Bay, Long Island, New York. He emigrated to Nova Scotia in October, 1783, with his wife and five children.

Stephen Dodge was born about 1748, died June 6, 1808, married Blanche Shaddon February 17, 1771, by whom he had nine children.

Sarah Dodge, born New York, November 24, 1771, died December 20, 1864.

Charles Dodge, born New York, September 18, 1773, died May 17, 1832.

Samuel Dodge, born New York, October 6, 1775, died June 6, 1852.

Mary Dodge, born New York, September 20, 1778, died 1845.

Freclove Dodge, born New York, March 24, 1781, died February, 1848.

Stephen Dodge (2d), born Granville, Nova Scotia, March 21, 1784, never married, died October 27, 1870.

Jacob Dodge, born Wilmot, Nova Scotia, November 26, 1786, died October 23, 1870.

John Dodge, born Wilmot, Nova Scotia, February 26, 1789, died July 18, 1875.

Isaac Dodge, born Wilmot, Nova Scotia, February 21, 1792, died December 21, 1878.

Sarah Dodge, born Wilmot, Nova Scotia.

Sarah Dodge married David Nichols, May 19, 1789, by whom she had seven children.

Sarah Nichols, born August 30, 1790, died 1819, married Robert Fitz Randolph, 1812. She left two sons and one daughter.

Mary Nichols, born July 20, 1792, died 1823, married the *above Robert Fitz* Randolph, 1820. She left one son and one daughter.

William Nichols, born October 22, 1794 (farmer), died February 15, 1881, married Phebe Young, by whom he had five children.

Amy Nichols, born October 22, 1797, married Henry D. Charlton (farmer), March 5, 1822, by whom she had six children, namely,

Eliza Charlton, born July 14, 1823, died February 6, 1829.

Edward C. Charlton, born February 14, 1825.

William H. Charlton, born December 17, 1826.

Ann Eliza Charlton, born November 2, 1831.

Mary Charlton, born July 22, 1833.

Randolph Charlton, born July 12, 1835. He is
master mariner.

Stephen Nichols, born December 16, 1799 (farmer), married Mary Rulofson, November 3,
1823, by whom he had six children, namely,

Amy Nichols, born July 31, 1824.

Seraphine Nichols, born March 2, 1826.

Rulof A. Nichols, born December 31, 1828.

William H. Nichols, born December 2, 1829.

David Nichols, born December 7, 1831.

Stephen James Nichols, born May 8, 1834.

Charles Dodge, master shipwright, and second
child of Stephen Dodge, married Mehettable
Gates, September 24, 1794, by whom he had
three children, namely,

Ambrose Dodge, born December 4, 1795, farmer,
died June 6, 1873, married Abigail Parker,
April 8, 1819, by whom he had eleven children, namely,

James P. Dodge, born September 20, 1820.

Samuel Dodge, born September 2, 1822, died October 17, 1840.

Obadiah Dodge, born November 21, 1824.

Keziah Dodge, born August 3, 1826, died January 25, 1866.

Susan M. Dodge, born July 31, 1828.

Hannah Dodge, born January 8, 1831, died January 27, 1849.

Isabel Dodge, born April 5, 1833.

Ingram B. Dodge, born March 11, 1835.

Charles E. Dodge, July 25, 1835.

Stephen A. Dodge, born May 27, 1839.

Robert Dodge, February 2, 1841.

Susannah Dodge, daughter of Charles Dodge, born December 16, 1797, died August 21, 1852, married Christopher Margeson, November 4, 1819, by whom he had eleven children, namely,

Bayard Margeson, born October 16, 1820 (carriage-maker and undertaker).

Ambrose Margeson, born July 12, 1822, died May 28, 1849.

Gilbert Margeson, born February 13, 1824 (blacksmith).

Parker Margeson, born November 2, 1826.

Thomas A. Margeson, born October 11, 1828 (merchant and justice of peace).

Harris H. Margeson, born October 31, 1830 (carriage-builder).

James Margeson, born September 7, 1832.

John Margeson, born February 17, 1835.

Lavinea Margeson, born March 6, 1837.

4

Christopher Margeson, born September 14, 1839.
Susannah Margeson, born October 11, 1842, died
July 19, 1865.

Maria Dodge, daughter of said Charles Dodge,
born April 25, 1800, married Robert Nichols
(farmer), by whom she has eleven children,
all married but one, and all with large families, and all living but the second daughter.

Charles Dodge's first wife (Mehettable) died April
15, 1802.
2d, married Margaret Rulofson, November 11,
1806, by whom he had ten children, namely,
Minetta Dodge, born September 19, 1808.
Helen Dodge, born September 27, 1810.
Mahettable Dodge, born January 1, 1813.
Emily Dodge, born February 27, 1815.
Charles R. Dodge, born April 18, 1817.
Louisa Dodge, born June 12, 1819, died August,
1880.
Amy A. Dodge, born April 19, 1821.
Lindley M. Dodge, born October 10, 1824.
William A. Dodge, born April 29, 1826.
James F. Dodge, born January 7, 1829.

Samuel Dodge, farmer and carpenter, married

Lydia Woodbury, January 26, 1806, by whom
he had ten children, namely,

Elizabeth Dodge, born September 17, 1806, married William H. Chipman, February 19, 1838,
by whom she had four children, namely,

Charlotte R. Chipman, born June 8, 1840.

Janet B. Chipman, born November 10, 1842.

Elizabeth R. Chipman, born September 23, 1845.

Harriet A. Chipman, born March 8, 1848.

Arthur Dodge, born November 9, 1808, wheel-
wright and undertaker, appointed justice of
peace, November, 1848, also town clerk and
treasurer for township of Wilmot in 1854, held
both offices ever since ; married Rebecca Chipman, May 24, 1832, by whom he had five
children, namely,

1. Samuel H. Dodge, born February 27, 1833
(carpenter and builder), married Mary North,
by whom he had five children, namely,

Louisa, Frank, Anthony, Eva, Rebecca.

2. Sarah E. Dodge, born July 7, 1837 (second
child of Arthur Dodge).

3. William W. Dodge, born November 20, 1843
(farmer and undertaker).

4. Annie A. Dodge, born October 14, 1846, married Handley Cheslay, farmer, December, 1877, by whom she had two children, namely,

Adda B. Cheslay, born January 17, 1879.

Edward Percy Cheslay, February 15, 1881.

5. Jessie R. Dodge, born December 2, 1850, died May 31, 1851.

3. Emily Dodge, born December 7, 1810, married Luther Morse, November 26, 1850, a farmer, no children.

4. John Dodge, born February 3, 1813, a farmer, married Harriet Woodbury, December 10, 1842, by whom he has two children, namely,

Ella Dodge, born January 26, 1845.

Albert Dodge, born March 10, 1847, married Adelia Bank, and has two children.

5. George Dodge, born February 22, 1815, a farmer, married Harriet Parker, February 14, 1846, by whom he has four children, namely,

Sophia Dodge, born November 15, 1848.

Beespe Dodge, born April 14, 1852.

Clara Dodge, born February 23, 1855.

Charles P. Dodge, born February 27, 1858.

6. Mary Dodge, born August 11, 1817, married

Zachariah Banks, carriage-builder, February
15, 1844, by whom she has three children,
namely,

Adelia Banks, born June 26, 1847.

Thomas Banks, born September 20, 1849.

Emma Banks, born August 15, 1852.

7. Edwin Gilpin Dodge, born December 19, 1819,
   a farmer, appointed justice of peace, 1848,
   married Keziah Dodge, December, 1849, by
   whom he had three children, namely,

Susan Alida Dodge, born July 10, 1851, died May
25, 1874.

Bessie C. Dodge, born April 4, 1854.

Willard P. Dodge, born November 3, 1858, died
October 14, 1878.

8. Charlotte Dodge, born November 6, 1822, married James P. Dodge, June 18, 1884, by whom
   she has three children, namely,

Edwin Dodge, born June 26, 1845.

Eugene and Augusta Dodge, born December 28,
1848.

9. Harriet Dodge, born May 15, 1825, married
   Obadiah Dodge, farmer, September, 1854, by
   whom she has three children, namely,

Abigail, Arthur P., and Carey.

10. Lavinea Dodge, born September 1, 1829, married Valentine Groop, January 15, 1855, by whom she has two children, namely,

Jessie B. and Minney.

Mary Dodge, fourth child of Stephen Dodge, married Elias Moore in 1804, by him had five children, namely,

Mary, Lindley M., Eliza, Elias, and Barah.

Freelove Dodge, fifth child of Stephen Dodge, married Isaac Longley, farmer, June, 1814, by whom she had four children, namely,

John, Darcus, Minetta, and

Jacob Dodge, master shipwright, seventh child of Stephen Dodge, married Rachel Clark, by whom he had five children, namely,

William, John, Maria, Mary, and Susan.

John Dodge, carriage-builder, eighth child of Stephen Dodge, married Mahettable Rulofson, December 3, 1818, by whom he had eight children, namely,

1. Ann Dodge, born April 19, 1820.

2. Alfred G. Dodge, born March 25, 1822, died

November 4, 1873, married January, 1851, and had five children, namely,

Ellen, Harry (a merchant), Rupert, Allice, and Hattie.

3. Priscilla Dodge, born June 20, 1822.

4. John A. Dodge, born November 21, 1826, died December 27, 1826.

5. Ethelinda Dodge, born March 10, 1828.

6. Isaiah Dodge, born May 3, 1830. Appointed justice of peace, 1878.

7. Arabel Dodge, born April 8, 1833.

8. Henrietta Dodge, born December 6, 1835.

Isaac Dodge, farmer and carpenter, ninth child of Stephen Dodge, married (1st) Letticia Charlton, July 8, 1815, by whom he had two children, namely,

Eveline Dodge, born April 19, 1816.

Edward Henry Dodge, born April 19, 1820, died December, 1824.

Isaac Dodge's 1st wife died November, 1821, married (2d) Grace Young, January, 1825, by whom he had three children, namely,

Henry Dodge, born January, 1826.

Wesley Dodge, born February, 1828.

Letticia Dodge, born June, 1829.

The present location of the lands at Cow Neck of Samuel Dodge is believed to be near the bounds of the farm of Richard Mott, Esq., which was lately of Joseph Dodge.

Wilkie Dodge, the witness to deed (1718) of Thomas Dodge and wife to Samuel Dodge, was the testator whose will is dated 1752, and father of my grandfather *Samuel;* his eldest son *Wilkie* was a captain in the West Indies trade.

He was a posthumous child, born after his father's death in 1750; master of a vessel during the Revolution, taken prisoner, and died in New York city about 1778.

I find on record in the office of the Surrogate of New York the following ancient wills, proved in the Probate Court of the Province, whose testators are above-named, viz. :

Tristram Dodge, dated October, 20, 1760.

Proved in Queens Co. 1760, December 29.

Rec. N. Y. Surv. Lib. 22, p. 313.

"Last will of Tristram Dodge of Cow Neck, Township of Hempstead, Queens Co., Province of New York."

After provision for his wife Phebe (formerly Phebe, widow of Adam Mott) : Devises all his real estate to his son Joseph Dodge.

CHAPTER V.

SAMUEL DODGE, *son of William Dodge* and
grandson of the original *settler Tristram*
Dodge, was born at New Shoreham or Block
Island, as appears by the record there, on
the 19th of September, 1691.

He was first cousin to the two preceding, viz.:
Thomas and Tristram Dodge, Jr.; settled at Cow
Neck prior to his arrival.

Samuel Dodge: first appears at Cow Neck, L. I.,
on the records of Hempstead, L. I., by the Deed of
Thomas Dodge and Susannah his wife of Hempstead, Queens County Province of New York—Yeoman To Samuel Dodge of the same place Yeoman. Dated 5, Gen. 1, and the "Year of man's Salvation (1718); Consideration £124; (Rec. 2, Lib. 2, p. 395) Conveys Farme att Hempstead of 59 acres 26 square Rods; or One Third, lacking Five acres of that Farme that was Samuel Clowes'; Bounded Easterdly, partly by Thomas Dodge aforesaid, and partly by Tristram Dodge, and northrdly by Rigbell Mott; westerly

by other lands laid out upon gate rights and
southrdly by the land belonging to the heirs of
John Carle deceased : "

Witnessed by

Thomas : (Jr) : Wilkie : ⎫
Trustom (3) Dodge   ⎭

In 1720, he is granted also :

Capt. John Cornell	"*Mai'd* ye 17th
of Cow Neck in town-	March, 1720 (Lib.
ship of Hempstead, Queen Co.	2, p. 397) Con. £500
Prov. of New York	of a Dwelling house
to	at Cow Neck nigh
Samual Dodge of the same	Cullards Cove, with
place, Yeoman	adjoining twenty
	acres of Land."

In 1731, *Samuel* is again granted at Cow Neck,
by same description ; by Deed :

Andrew Onderdonk of Cow Neck
Hempstead, Queens Co. Pro. N. Y., Yeoman

and Gertry his wife	Dated 12 April
to	in the year of
Samuel Dodge of the same place,	Our Lord Christ
Yeoman.	1731.
	Con. £274 12s.
	Lib. 2, p. 392.

Conveys: "a piece of land on Cow Neck; bounded Easterly by the highway that leads through ye Neck; Northerly by the Highway that leads to Landing; Westwardly by Land of Robert Hutchings and Jonathan Whitehead, Southerly by land of Andrew Onderdonk; containing Fifty-three acres ¾ and 36 rods" (with a survey description).

Will of *Tristram "Dodge"* (3) of ye Township "of Oyster Bay; Queens Co. Nassau Island and Colony of New York." Died 1760.

1. After his .wife's death Devises all his Real Estate in "Equal Halfs" to his sons *Daniel* and *Stephen* Dodge, and then makes the following bequests

2. To my daughter Sarah—one feather bed.

3. To   do.   Freelove (wife of Townsend Parish) same; and to do. Sarah and Anne the personalty in equal shares.

———

Will of *Wilkie Dodge* (son of Samuel—son of William Dodge who was *son of Tristram* (1).
Will dated Feb. 13, 1752—Rec. Lib. 18, p. 148 of "Wilkie Dodge of Flushing, Queens Co. on Nassau Island, Province of New York."

First Devises " to *my son Samuel*, lot of land at Cow Neck, Nassau Island, near the land of my father joining to the Creek."

Bequeaths to his daughter Sarah, and to his youngest son, Jesse, each—certain silver plate.

Appoints as executors his father Samuel Dodge and his brother Samuel Dodge and Mary Dodge, wife.

He was interred in the Quaker burial-ground at Cow Neck.

Will of *Samuel Dodge :* (father of said Wilkie born at Block Island, 1691, as above).

Dated New York, May 23, 1761. Proved N. Y., ——, 1766. Lib. 23, p. 28.

After bequests for her life to his wife Elizabeth :

2. Devises Lot of land in Queen St. to his *son Jeremiah ;* do. next Lot do. do. do. Samuel.

3. His whole estate (except as follows) to his said two sons and daughter Deborah.

4 To his grandson, *Samuel*, son of Wilkie (deceased), " all that ground in Cow Neck, L. I., near the house of Joseph Dodge, lying on the South side of the road, that leads from said house up the Neck between said road and the farm of Oliver Baxter, be it more or less."

His *grandson Samuel Dodge*, son of *Wilkie* as
above, was the Author's *grandfather*, and of the
fourth generation in *descent from Tristram* (1), *the
original settler of Block Island.*

In this historic narrative the scene now changes
to Ulster County, State of New York, Township
of *Marbletown*, where it continues during part of
the war of the American Revolution, and finally
to the city of New York.

Ulster County, New York, in 1683, by the Colonial Governor, Lovelace, was organized by Charter
dated 1st November, "to contain the towns of
Kingston, Hurley, Marbletown, Foxhall, and the
New Paltz, with all villages, neighborhoods, and
Christian inhabitants, from the Murderer's Creek
near the Highlands to the Sawyer's Creek."

Orange County, formed also in 1683, comprises
all the region West of Hudson River and South of
Murderer's Creek.

Both counties were then the wilderness frontier,
and without any attempt at settled boundaries, till
1774, and the Colonial Act "To run the boundary
of Ulster and Orange County, from the East side of
the Shawangunk Mountains to the Delaware River."
Ulster County included the country generally be-

tween the Hudson and Delaware Rivers. In 1797, part of Delaware County; 1800, part of Green County; 1809, part of Sullivan County were annexed; and in 1798, part of Ulster County was annexed to Orange County.

By 1809 the two counties attained their present bounds.

During the Revolutionary period, that ensued so soon after the first colonial act (1774), " to run the boundary between Ulster and Orange Counties," there was no time to survey and map boundaries of the vast unexplored wilderness called " Ulster," from his native county in Ireland, by Gov. Lovelace, at the same time when he took possession for James II., Duke of York, of the Dutch fort " *Ronduit*," on Hudson River, and their walled town, which he named " Kingston," and the next Dutch " Nieuw Dorp," that he named " Hurley:" both from his home in Ireland.

In fact, throughout the Revolution, the two counties formed one; the inhabitants of Ulster being designated as of Orange County, and those of Orange called of Ulster County.

Marbletown was patented June 25, 1703, to Col. Henry Beekman and associates—*thirteen* in all— who held all the lands in common, till surveys and allotments made were filed under the State law of 1783. The town was organized in 1788.

It was an old settlement at the time of the Revolution, but with undefined boundaries. There was no other settlement south of it to the Delaware River; and until long after the Revolution *Marbletown* was the name of the whole unexplored frontier region of Ulster County, extending along the Esopus and Rondout creeks. The origin of the name is from the large deposit of a very hard white limestone there, still abundant, and in those days reputed to be a good building *marble*.

This town now lies on the old High Road south-west from the city of Kingston, to the Delaware River, along the Isthmus of fertile farms between the Rondout and Esopus creeks; in their Valley guarded on the west by the Shawangunk Range; and on the east by the Shandaken or lower Catskill Mountains.

The settlement was on Rondout and Esopus creeks. The mountains were the war-paths of the hostile Indians; of whom the Six Nations, under their chief (of the Mohawks), Joseph Brandt, were subsidized through the brutal policy of the British Government, by treaty with Sir Guy Carleton at Montreal, Governor of Canada, through the price of

a guinea for each white scalp delivered there; to
every extent of murder and rapine in their stealthy
and frequent raids upon the scattered settlers of the
frontier valleys.

The family record of the parents of my grandfather, which he must have had, is now lost; perhaps in their burning home in Rondout Valley.

His life-period was perhaps from 1740–1800, and
he was doubtless born at Cow Neck on the homestead farm of his grandfather, whose name he
bore.

He married *Deborah*, daughter of Dr. Robert
North, of Dutchess County, New York (born in
London, England), about 1769, and settled in
Marbletown, Ulster County.

By contemporary evidence from a deed by John
Allen and wife to Robert North (1764), of a lot of
land in Rosevelt Street, New York City, witnessed
by Samuel Dodge, my grandfather and his father-
in-law were inhabitants of New York City in 1764;
where probably the marriage, whose evidence is lost,
occurred.

Samuel Dodge, my grandfather, with his wife
were early settlers in Marbletown, upon the banks
of Rondout Creek not far from Hurley; and here

his earlier children were born. The six children
subsequent to 1779 were born in New York City.

At Marbletown.

Wilkie Dodge, born 1771.

Mary	"	1773, August 9.
Daniel	"	1775, April 5.
Moses	"	1777, January 5.

Robert—my father—1779, April 17;
    died 1825, December 14, at New York.

At New York City.

James	born	1781, April 8.
Andrew	"	1783, June 4.
Katharine	"	1785, October.
Margaret	"	1787, February 2.
Charles	"	1790, March 25.
Katharine (2)	"	1792, January 16.

All of those, now deceased, left no surviving representatives.

Grandfather had been long married, and settled
in Marbletown, when the first shot at Lexington,
Massachusetts, April 19, 1775, was fired "around
the world."

"Upon tidings of the battle of Lexington," says
Colonel Marinus Willett, in his narrative (1795) of

"Proceedings in New York City," "the most active of the citizens formed themselves into a voluntary corps, assumed the command of the city, and possessed themselves of the keys of the custom house and public stores.

"There was a general stagnation of business; armed citizens constantly paraded about the city without any definite object. The British garrison was confined to their barracks (in the Park), etc. The unsystematic and confused manner in which things were conducted manifested the necessity of forming some regular plan of government; to effect which a meeting of the citizens was requested at the merchant's coffee-house; where it was unanimously agreed that the government should be placed in the hands of a committee, and solemn resolutions entered into to support these measures until further provision should be made by the Continental Congress which was shortly to meet in Philadelphia.

"The sacred honor of the citizens being pledged at the same time to support the measures of Congress. A committee of one hundred citizens was then formed and the pledge of Association generally signed."

Gaine's New York *Gazette and Weekly Mercury*, for Monday, May 1, 1775, says:

" The following Association was set on foot here last Saturday (April 29), and on that day it was signed by one hundred of our principal inhabitants. It is to be transmitted to all the counties in the province, where we make no doubt it will be signed by all ranks of people."

(Annexing a copy of the following General Association.)

"Calendar of Papers and MSS. of the Revolution, N. Y., 1868.

"General Association,"
Goshen, Orange Co.
April 29, 1775.

"A general association agreed to and submitted by the Freeholders and Inhabitants of the County of Orange in the Province of New York.

"Persuaded that the salvation of the rights and liberties of America depends, under God, on the firm union of its inhabitants, in a vigorous prosecution of the measures necessary for its safety; and convinced of the necessity of preventing the anarchy and confusion which attend a dissolution of the powers of government: We, the freemen, freeholders, and inhabitants of the County of Orange, being greatly alarmed at the avowed designs of the ministry to raise a revenue in America, and shocked by the bloody scenes now acting in Massachusetts Bay: Do, in the most solemn manner, resolve never to become slaves, and do associate, under all the ties of religion, honor, and love to our country; to adopt, and endeavor to carry into execution whatever measures may be recommended by the Continental Congress, or resolved upon by the Provincial Congress, for the purpose of preserving our constitution, and opposing the execution of the several arbitrary and oppressive acts of the British Parliament, until a reconciliation between Great Britain and America on constitutional principles (which we most ardently desire) can be obtained; and that we will in all things follow the advice of our respective committees respecting the purposes aforesaid, the preservation of peace and good order and the safety of individuals and private property.

"Adopted in Marbletown, Ulster Co.

5 June, 1775.

Levi Pawling,
Chairman.

"Signed
(with many others)
Samuel Dodge."

In the same Calendar we also find the following petition :

"PETITION FROM MARBLETOWN, ULSTER COUNTY.

"MARBLETOWN, *March*, 1776.
" To the Hon. the Provincial Congress for the Province of New York:

" The petition of Josiah Robertson, Johannis Tack and others, of Marbletown, in the county of Ulster, Province of New York, Humbly sheweth, that whereas the Township of Marbletown, formerly contained a sufficient number of men for three distinct companies of militia, which although increased since that time, was by the committee of said town, for local convenience only, divided into two beats or districts, and now form two companys of upwards of one hundred men each. And whereas certain dissatisfactions have arisen about the choice of a Capt" in the Southwest district of said Township, which we humbly conceive may have an evil tendency to disunite the good people of this town, if some suitable remedy be not applied in time. And whereas it is judged that the most effectual method for removing dissatisfactions from among us would be for to raise a Company of Grenadiers, under the command of Charles W. Brodhead, Capt.,

Jacob Delamater, 1st Lieutenant, Moses M. Cantine, 2d Lieutenant, and Jacob Chambers, Ensign.

We therefore having obtained the previous ap-
probation of the commanding officer of this Regiment, together with ye Committee and ye officers
of ye militia of said township, Humbly pray that
we may be imbodyed into a company of Grenadiers
in said Regiment and that the said Charles W.
Brodhead, Jacob Delamater, Moses M. Cantine and
Jacob Chambers may be commissioned as above
mentioned, and your Petitioners shall ever pray."

(Signed with 69 others, whose representatives are
still inhabitants of Marbletown) by

Samuel Dodge.

(Indorsed March 20, 1776.) "Petition of the
Marbletonians. They are grown to the stature of
Grenadiers. Let them be commanded as such by
Charles W. Brodhead. Amen."

In 1778 *said Samuel Dodge* signs the petition to
Gov. George Clinton, of the inhabitants of Roches-
ter, then lately organized from Marbletown, for protection against the Indians.

The organization of the Revolutionary American
armies was very imperfect and but few traces remain. It is believed that these Grenadiers were

soon mustered into service and marched to join Gen. Gates at Saratoga, in which victory grandfather shared, and continued with the army till after 1779, when he returned to New York City, where he died.

Robert Dodge, my father, was born as above at Marbletown, Ulster County, New York, April 17, 1779; and in August ensuing his mother fled with him, her infant fifth child, on a raft upon the Rondout Creek and Hudson River at night, their path lighted by the flames of their cottage that perished amid the yells of the savages and Tories, to his future home—New York City; in which he was reared and passed his life. His mother was alone in her hour of trial; grandfather being absent on duty in the army under General Gates. She took with her all her five children, the oldest being only of eight years. Grandfather joined them in New York City soon after, on leaving the army.

The plundering and burning raid of the Indians and Tories had destroyed nearly all the family property; and the nurture and education of a large family was due to their sterling energy and thrift.

"Robert learned his trade." In those early days, few began life with any other resource; and the

founders of the best of our city families, now conspicuous for antiquity and wealth, were mostly mechanics.   His fellow-apprentices were Gerardus and
William Post, Stephen Allen, John Targee, Jacob
Harsen, and many other equally well-known and honored citizens, who achieved their own fortunes and
high stations as the just reward of their useful lives.

Father was an officer of the City Artillery
stationed at Fort Green in 1812; also an active
life-long member of the Mechanics' Society and of
the Volunteer Fire Department of the city; assistant foreman of Company No. 15, to Mr. Peterson,
and his successor; also of the Society of Tammany
at its origin, when representing the spirit and pre-
cepts of Jefferson and Tompkins.

In the New York City Directory (vol. 23) for
1812–13 is an appendix, in which, as advertisement,
is a very copious account of the origin, purposes,
and organization of the Tammany Society, their
processions, celebrations, etc., signed by all the
officers and Sachems in their quaint style and titles.

Sachem of the South Carolina or Raccoon Tribe
Robert Dodge.

On the same page appears Stephen Allen as Sachem of the New Jersey or Tortoise Tribe.

It is part of our earliest civic memories how these honored fathers appeared as Sachems in Indian bravery, leading the hosts of Tammany's warriors in many a city procession and pageant.

He was conspicuous in devotion to duty in every relation, and especially as an officer in the Fire Department, at the first fire of the old Park Theatre, and the wide desolation, in 1811, of the great fire in Chatham Street, where he led his men into the seething flames repeatedly, saving lives and property. To such fearless exposure and self-sacrifice might be attributed the paralysis which so early (1824) checked his manly vigor and fatally terminated his life after a year's illness, December 14, 1825, in his forty-seventh year.

Robert Dodge and *Eliza Pollock Fowler* were married at New York City, January 3d, 1801.
Children :
Ellen R. Dodge, born 1801, October 16; died 1802, September 23.
Samuel N. Dodge, born 1802, December 4 ; died 1865, April 14.
Mary E. Dodge, born 1804, November 17 ; died 1885, November 2.
Robert and William, born 1806, September 20 ;

died, Robert, 1807, January 8; William, 1864,
July 12.

George R. Dodge, born 1809, February 20; died
1866, August.

Robert E. Dodge, born 1811, September 20; died
1812, August 10.

Martha A. Dodge, born 1813, January 17.

Henry S. Dodge, born 1815, November 12; died
1855, September 17.

John R. Dodge, born 1818, May, 16; died 1828,
September 2.

Robert Dodge, born 1820, December 15.

———

Eliza P. Dodge, my venerated mother, whose honored membership of the Baptist Church in New York City for over fifty years, as well as her model life of beneficence, made her so widely known and beloved, was born at Bayside, near Flushing, Long Island, on the 10th day of September, 1783, and she died in New York City, 10th November, 1863.

She wore the silver crown of eighty years for just two months—" when she was not, for God took her."

Their sons have proved not unworthy.

Samuel North Dodge was for some years President of the Seventh Ward Bank, New York City, and few in the busy city attached a larger circle of valued friends.

George Riker Dodge long resided in Baltimore, where he died. He was a prominent Unionist there, when, in the late Civil War, the rebels in that city sought to draw Maryland into the Confederacy. On July 10, 1861, by order of General Banks, in command, he was appointed Marshal of Police, or Provost Marshal at Baltimore; and by the order of General Banks's successor, Major-General John A. Dix, he arrested the Mayor of the city and the delegates to the State Legislature, and saved the city and State in the Union.

Scharff's History of Maryland, vol. 3, pp. 439–41, says:

"Gen. N. P. Banks, in command at Fort McHenry.

"BALTIMORE, *July* 10, 1861.

"By virtue of authority vested in me, as commanding officer of this Department, I have appointed, and do hereby appoint, George R. Dodge, Esquire, of Baltimore, Marshal of Police: and Colonel John R. Kenly, who, being relieved of this service, at his own request, now assumes command of the First Regiment of Maryland Volunteers, on the Upper Potomac, in the State of Maryland.

"N. P. BANKS,
"U. S. Maj.-Gen."

"The appointment of Mr. Dodge, as Provost Marshal of Baltimore, was accompanied by the withdrawal of the troops from the central part of the city; and from that time until the restoration of peace, the Police Department of Baltimore was under the military power of the Federal Government."

"TO GEORGE R. DODGE, ESQ.,
"Provost Marshal.

"12 *September*, 1861.

"Arrest without one hour's delay: George William Brown, Mayor of Baltimore, and the within named delegates to the Legislature.

"JNO. A. DIX,
"U. S. Maj.-Gen."

Henry Swartwout Dodge was a distinguished member of the Bar of New York City, and, from excessive professional labor, died in his fortieth year.

Samuel North Dodge married (1837) Clara Whiting, sister of the late Hon. James R. Whiting, eminent as District Attorney and Justice of the Supreme Court of New York.

Their eldest daughter, Clara, is wife of Henry Morton, Ph.D., President of the Stevens Institute of Technology, Hoboken, N. J., and of much scientific repute.

Mrs. Eliza P. Gibson, widow, her sister, are all that survive of his family.

Henry Swartwout Dodge married (1836) Mary
  D. L. M. Moore (died 1848); he died September 17, 1855, leaving his daughter, Katharine
  Alice Dodge, and his son, Henry M. Dodge,
  who married (1880) Annie B. Keeler. One
  child, Harold Dodge.
Robert Dodge married (May 16, 1867) M. Annie
  Roe, daughter of the late Charles Roe, Bayside, Long Island.
Martha Ann Dodge married (August 9, 1841) A. L.
  DeCamp, only surviving child, R. L. DeCamp.
Wilkie Dodge (father of my grandfather) and his
  wife, Mary (daughter of Thomas Hunt, of
  Hunt's Point, Westchester County, New
  York, born 1725), died, New York, July 23,
  1796.

Children:

Samuel.

Wilkie, died 1778, at Hunt's Point.

Sarah, born May 24, 1749, died, New York, January 24, 1795, interred at St. Paul's, East Chester, married (June 3, 1769) Comfort Sands, who was early prominent as a Whig patriot of New York City, and merchant, Commissary General of the Revolutionary Army and Commissioner of Accounts.

Wilkie Dodge died at Cow Neck, Long Island. He was a ship-builder at Whitestone (town of Flushing, Long Island) for many years, where he lived till shortly before his death (by consumption), he moved to Cow Neck.

Comfort Sands, born at Cow Neck, Long Island, early settled as a merchant in New York City, and was active in resisting the British oppression. In 1765, on the arrival at Burling Slip of the brig from London, bringing the first cargo of stamps, he aided in removing her bales of stamped papers in the night, and in taking them to the beach of Colonel Rutger's farm (now Seventh Ward), East River, where they were burned.

1774. Member of the first Continental Congress

and one of Committee of Sixty, to secure compliance with their resolutions of non-importation.

1775. On the tidings of the conflict at Lexington reaching New York City, by the meeting of citizens, he was appointed and served on the Committee of One Hundred, to see to the "execution of the non-importation resolve, and provide for the public safety."

In 1776, the Non-Importation Association with his signature was published.

1775, November 7, he was elected to the Provincial Congress, serving until June 30, 1776, and also as one of the pay table, and on the Committee of Safety. In 1776, appointed Auditor General of the State of New York, serving until 1782.

1777. One of the Commissioners appointed by the Continental Congress for New York to meet at New Haven with members from other States, to regulate prices of articles for army.

He was baptized and communed in St. Paul's Church, New York City, in 1767, the year of its erection, and was its oldest member at his death in 1834 (in Hoboken, New Jersey).

1784. On the organization of the "Bank of New

York," March 17, 1784, he was chosen on the first Board of Directors. It was then the only bank in the city; and, relatively, the Directors were like Governors of the Bank of England.

CHAPTER VI.

JEREMIAH DODGE, brother of Wilkie, above named, and uncle of my grandfather, born at Cow Neck, Long Island, May, 1716, died at New York City, 1800, married October 6, 1737, Margaret Vanderbilt (born 1718; died, New York, 1804).

True to ancestral faith, Jeremiah Dodge planted the first Baptist Church in New York City. Dr. Robert North, from London, and Samuel Dodge, of my kindred, joined with him from the outset.

In 1745, at the house of Jeremiah Dodge, in New York City, the Baptists first gathered in prayer meetings, at which Dr. Robert North and a few more regularly attended every week. He and Dr. North invited the Rev. John Pyne, of Fishkill, to preach to their meeting, and he officiated till his death, 1750; when they united with the church at Scotch Plains, New Jersey, and its pastor, Rev. Benjamin Miller, preached to them at intervals from 1753. The assembly increased so much that they

6

hired a larger room in a rigging-loft in Cart and
Horse Lane (now William Street, from Fulton to
John Street) for one year, after which they continued their meetings at the house of Joseph Meeks
for a year.

In 1760, they bought part of a lot on Golden
Hill (John Street).

In 1762, the *first* or earliest Baptist Church of
New York City was organized with about twenty
members, in the Golden Hill Meeting-House.

Jeremiah Dodge, .

Dr. Robert North,

Samuel Dodge, and

Margaret Dodge, its first members, are justly to
be recorded as the Patriarch founders of the denomination in New York City.

Their first pastor was the Rev. Stephen Gano.
He was a leading patriot, and early became Chaplain
in the Revolutionary Army, New York Line, serving until the Peace. In 1787 (according to a letter
from New York City, by Hon. William Grayson to
James Monroe, 22d October, 1787), " Rev. Dr. Gano,
with his whole congregation, about five hundred,
would, it was said, early leave to settle in the new
lands of the Ohio purchase."

Dr. Gano, with some associates, soon after settled

in the Ohio purchase, where he lived till his death. The society remained.

The Records of the present First Baptist Church, New York City, begin on June 12, 1762, and of those members of the church at Scotch Plains dismissed, as above stated, to form the above church in New York City, are :

Jeremiah Dodge,

Samuel Dodge, and

Margaret Dodge, who sign Covenant on organization June 19, 1762.

Samuel Dodge (born 1730) was chosen clerk, and Rev. Stephen Gano, pastor.

From its locality, it was then popularly known as the "Golden Hill Baptist Meeting."

1770. June 4.

Jeremiah Dodge, ⎫   Dismissed to form Second
Margaret Dodge, ⎬   Baptist Church, N. Y. City,
Samuel Dodge,   ⎭   in Fayette, now Oliver St.

Samuel Dodge, baptized 1756.

Margaret Dodge, "   1805, August 6.

Eliza P. Dodge,   "   1810, June 6, in the First Baptist Church, and on February 10, 1812, dismissed, at their request, to unite with the (Second) Baptist Church in Fayette (Oliver) Street, whose pastor was the Rev. John Williams, father of the late Rev. Dr. W. R. Williams.

Jeremiah Dodge, born May, 1716, died in N. Y., 1800.

Married, October 6, 1737,

Margaret Vanderbilt, born 1718, died April, 1804.

Rev. John Dodge, Pleasant Valley, Dutchess Co., N. Y., born February 22, 1738, died April 13, 1816.

Samuel Dodge, born August 9, 1758, died October 20, 1820.

Jeremiah Dodge, born October 15, 1755, died September 24, 1813.

Margaret Dodge, born July 23, 1745, died April, 1823.

Marcia Dodge, born January 12, 1751.

Mary Dodge, born June 7, 1753, died October 21, 1755.

Elizabeth Dodge.

Rev. John Dodge (Baptist), born February 22, 1738, died April 13, 1816.

Thrice married: 1st, married, December 23, 1759,

Elizabeth Denton, born September 30, 1741, died March 8, 1762.

Jeremiah Dodge, M.D., Dutchess Co., N. Y., born May 18, 1761, died September 11, 1842.

2d, Married, February 7, 1763,

Annie Smith, born April 2, 1741, died May 13, 1774.

Anna Dodge, born December 27, 1763, died September 1, 1764.

John Dodge, born October 7, 1768, died October 16, 1768.

Phineas Dodge, born February 2, 1772, died June 16, 1772.

3d, Married, October 13, 1777,

Keziah Newcomb, born November 7, 1758, died February 1, 1814.

John Dodge, M.D., Clinton, N. Y., born July 7, 1778, died October 27, 1849.

Samuel K. Dodge, Honesdale, Pa., born October 12, 1779, died September 12, 1863.

Elizabeth Dodge, born June 29, 1782, died June 29, 1855.

David S. Dodge, Alton, Ill., born December 23, 1783, died November 2, 1872.

Margaret Dodge, born February 27, 1786, died August 8, 1788.

Sarah Dodge, born March 17, 1788, died April, 1874.

Marcia Dodge, born August 16, 1790, died September 11, 1854.

Adam T. Dodge, Brooklyn, N. Y., born July 23,
1792, died October 8, 1872.

Cyrenius N. Dodge, New York, born August 13,
1794, died February 14, 1863.

Margaret Dodge, born December 21, 1796, died
December 25, 1850.

Edwin Dodge, died Grand Gulf, Miss., born December 21, 1798, died October 9, 1836.

Keziah Dodge, born February 17, 1801, died 1865.

Samuel Dodge, born August 9, 1758,
        Married
Ann Stansbury, of Baltimore, Md.
                            No children.

Jeremiah Dodge, born October 15, 1755, died
September 24, 1813.
        Married
Sarah Frost, born February 26, 1762, died No-
vember 29, 1824.

John Dodge, born May 18, 1779, died December
6, 1831.

Jeremiah Dodge, born July 23, 1781, died January
11, 1860.

Samuel Dodge.

Margaret Dodge, born October 23, 1787,
Susan Dodge.

Adam Todd, born June 2, 1746,
> Married

Margaret Dodge, born July 23, 1745, died April,
> 1823.

David Stodder, 2d,
> Married

Marcia Dodge, born January 12, 1751.

William Halleck
> Married

Elizabeth Dodge.

Jeremiah Dodge, born May 18, 1761, died September 11, 1842.
> Married

Esther Lane.

David L. Dodge, born February 21, 1790, died
> October 6, 1873.

Benjamin Dodge died single.
John Dodge,
Elizabeth Dodge.

John Dodge, born July 7, 1778, died October 27,
> 1849.

Thrice married ; 1st, married, October 26, 1803,.

Sallie M. Hawkins, born October 19, 1788, died April 10, 1811.

Joseph Dodge, born July 15, 1804, died April 9, 1808.

Keziah C. Dodge, born May 7, 1806, died May 6, 1872.

Jeremiah Edwin Dodge, Lancaster, Wis., born February 20, 1809, died 1877.

2d, married, December 22, 1811,

Sophia Cheesman, born May 21, 1792, died October 11, 1827.

Nathaniel Dodge, born February 21, 1813, died December 21, 1813.

John Dodge, M.D., Grant Co., Wis., born November 5, 1816, died March 14, 1869.

Cheesman F. Dodge, N. Y., born March 22, 1817.

Samuel Dodge, M.D., Poughkeepsie, born August 26, 1819, died June 30, 1863.

Margaret Dodge, born October 16, 1821.

Robert L. Dodge, Judge Common Pleas, Kingston, Mo., born November 16, 1823.

David Dodge, Esq., Kerwin, Kansas, born January 20, 1826.

3d, married, December 18, 1828,

Mehetable Mosher, born November 13, 1810, died January 27, 1841.

Sarah Dodge, born September 2, 1829.

Marcia E. Dodge, born March 29, 1831, died November 27, 1878.

Benjamin Franklin Dodge, born July 15, 1832, died Holly Springs, Miss., 1856.

Abraham Dodge, born July 22, 1838, died 1863, killed in battle, last war, 10th Reg. Wis. Vol.

Samuel S. Dodge, born October 12, 1779.

Stephen Dubois
   Married
Sarah Dodge, born March 17, 1788, died April, 1874.

Robert Lawrence
   Married
Marcia Dodge, born August 16, 1790, died September 11, 1854.

William Wilder
   Married
Keziah Dodge, born February 17, 1801, died 1865.

Edwin Dodge, born December 21, 1798, died October 9, 1836.
   Married,   1st,

Annabella Dodge.   .

David L. Dodge, born February 21, 1790, died
   October 6, 1873.
   Married
Mary Flagler, born January 31, 1793, died March
   13, 1869.
Catharine M. Dodge, born July 13, 1813.
John A. Dodge, born October 16, 1818, died New
   York, 1881.

George Mosher
   Married
Catharine M. Dodge, born July 13, 1813.

John A. Dodge, born October 16, 1818, died
   1881.
   Married, 1st,
Annie S. Brown, who died leaving son,

Henry C. Dodge,
   Married, 2d,
Parthenia J. Stevenson.

William S. Dodge,	died
Annie Dodge,	died
John Dodge,	died
William D. Dodge,	died
Mary F. Dodge,	

Richard H. Dodge,
Elizabeth H. Dodge,
Cornelia A. Dodge,
Edward L. Dodge.

Henry C. Dodge, eldest above, at the age of six-teen years, was appointed Cadet in the U. S. Military Academy, West Point, graduating in June, 1864; he was, as 2d Lieutenant, ordered to U. S. 2d Artillery of the Potomac Army under Gen. Grant, and served till the end of the war, and one year in garrison at Fort Riley, Kansas. In 1870, the Second Artillery was ordered to the Pacific Coast. He had been promoted Captain, and was stationed at Portland, Oregon; and was thence ordered to Sitka, in Alaska, where he remained in command for about a year and a half, when his regiment being ordered to the Atlantic Coast, was relieved by the 3d Artillery at Sitka. Captain Dodge was detained, to turn over the U. S. property to his successor, until January, 1873, when he left Sitka for Portland, in Oregon, on the steamer George H. Wright; which was never heard from, but is supposed to have been lost in a violent storm on her passage through Queen Charlotte Sound. A revenue cutter in search found fragments of wreck along the Sound, and learned

from the Indians of the coast that some U. S. officers
and men, escaping from a steamer wrecked in the
Sound, had been killed by the native savages.

The New York *Times* of November 30, 1881,
contains the following notice of the death of John
A. Dodge:

"Col. John A. Dodge (John A. Dodge & Co.,
Bankers, No. 12 Wall Street), died at his residence
No. 116 E. 52d Street on 28th inst. He had been
ailing since September last, but only for two weeks
since confined to his bed. He was born near Poughkeepsie, N. Y., Oct. 16, 1818, and at 17 years settled at Springport, near Auburn, N. Y., as a merchant, until the outbreak of the rebellion in 1861.
He was then Lieut.-Colonel 49th Regiment, N. Y.
S. M., risen from a private by long service in every
rank. He at once raised the 57th Regiment, N. Y.
Volunteers, was commissioned its Colonel, and led
it to Santa Rosa, Florida, where it was on duty during the greater portion of its time of service. He
took part in the bombardment of Pensacola, Fla.,
and many skirmishes. Ill health obliged him to
ask for discharge; but this was refused from the
Government's need of his efficient service. He was
transferred to Hilton Head, S. C.; but continuing
to fail rapidly, was relieved from duty, and returned

to Auburn, where he organized and became President of the Dodge and Stevenson Manufacturing Company of Mowers, Reapers, etc. He retired in 1873, and came to New York, engaging as a banker. His death was from malarial fever contracted in the war. He leaves a widow, three daughters, and two sons. Funeral on Friday, 2d Dec. ; buried at Fort Hill Cemetery, Auburn, N. Y."

John Wilber, born July 7, 1802,
    Married (1825, December 15)
Keziah C. Dodge, born May 7, 1806, died May 1,
    1872.
Edwin J. Wilber, born December 30, 1826.
Mark D. Wilber, born August 12, 1829. U. S.
    District Attorney, E. D. N. Y. (1886).
John W. Wilber, born   , 1834.
Jeremiah E. Dodge, born February 20, 1809, died
    ——, 1877.
    Married (1834), 1st,
Rosanna Ashley,   died   , 1838.
    Married (1843), 2d,
Rachel M. Ashley.
Rosanna Dodge,
Wilber Dodge,
Jeremiah Dodge.

John Dodge, born November 5, 1816, died March
14, 1867.
Married
Catharine E. Perrin.
Edwin Dodge,
Sarah Dodge,
John Dodge,
William Dodge,
Frank Dodge,
Lizzie Dodge.

Cheesman Dodge, born March 22, 1817,
Married Catharine Darling.

Samuel Dodge, born August 26, 1817, died January 30, 1863.
Married Miss Rome, child, Clarence Dodge.

Milton Woolley married, December 15, 1839,
Margaret Dodge, born October 6, 1820.
Myron Woolley,
Robert D. Woolley,
William W. Woolley,
John J. Woolley,
Mary Woolley,
Martha Woolley,
Rachel Woolley,

Eliza J. Woolley,
John M. Woolley.   ·

Robert L. Dodge, born November 16, 1823,
    Married, 2d,
Laura Kantz,   .
David Dodge, born January 20, 1826.

Elmer Fitch
    Married
Sarah Dodge, born September 2, 1829.

George A. Vanderwater
    Married·   ·
Marcia E. Dodge, born March 29, 1831.

Samuel Dodge, born August 9, 1758, second son
of Jeremiah, as above, enlisted at the age of sixteen
in the Revolutionary Army.

He became Ensign in the 4th New York Conti-
nentals and was at the battle of Saratoga.

At the close of the war in 1783 he signed at New-
burgh, New York, the Institution of the Society of
the Cincinnati as Ensign.

He married Ann Stansbury, of Baltimore, Md.,
of which port he was appointed Collector. He left
no issue.

His cousin, of same name, born September, 1754,

hereinafter mentioned, also signed the Institution of the Cincinnati as Captain. The latter left one child, his son, Henry S. Dodge, who died in 1841.

David S. Dodge, born December 23, 1784, died November 7, 1872, married

Nancy Rice, born July 6, 1784, died June 30, 1851.

Charles E. Dodge, born February 9, 1810, died April 17, 1875.

John Dodge, born October 14, 1811, died September 26, 1812.

Mary Dodge, born August 11, 1813.

Rev. Henry W. Dodge, born November 16, 1815.

Harriet Dodge, born August 14, 1818, died May 24, 1847.

Margaret Dodge, born January 29, 1821, died April 27, 1860.

John P. Dodge, born March 18, 1824.

Egbert Dodge, born October 4, 1826.

Charles E. Dodge, born February 9, 1810, died April 17, 1875.

Mary Dodge, born August 11, 1813.

Rev. Henry W. Dodge, born November 16, 1815, Married, 1st,

A. R. Brown, born July 23, 1816, died July 10, 1864.

Mary E. Dodge, born August 19, 1840, died August 25, 1841.

William E. Dodge, born February 21, 1843, died October 17, 1844.

Daniel B. Dodge, born December 12, 1844, died March 1, 1853.

Margaret D. Dodge, born December 26, 1846.

Mary E. Dodge, born December 5, 1848, died June 19, 1851.

Henry W. Dodge, Jr., born

Sarah E. Dodge, born November 15, 1853, died 1864.

Egbert M. Dodge, born 1863, died 1864.

   Married, July 12, 1865,

Mrs. Ida B. Latham.

Clarence P. Dodge, born March 13, 1867.

William R. Dodge, born November, 1870.

William F. Kerfoot

   Married, October 6, 1870,

Margaret D. Dodge, born December 26, 1846.

Maria M. Kerfoot, born May 30, 1872.

Daniel B. Kerfoot, born May 12, 1874.

Susan E. Kerfoot, born October 12, 1878.

Samuel K. Dodge, born October 12, 1779, died September 12, 1863.

Married, March, 1805, 1st wife,
Hannah Cons, died March 10, 1806.

Keziah Dodge, born January 8, 1806, died July
30, 1863.
Married, September 9, 1807, 2d wife,
Isabella Balding, died May 7, 1820.
John S. Dodge, born August 14, 1808.
David E. Dodge, born February 14, 1811.
William Dodge, born April 20, 1813.
Cyrenius M. Dodge, born May 8, 1816.
George E. Dodge, born December 28, 1818.

Married, March 10, 1831, 3d wife,
Fanny Huntington, died June 23, 1870.
No children.

Peter Pulis
Married
Keziah Dodge, born January 8, 1806, died July
30, 1863.

John S. Dodge, born August 14, 1808,
Married
Emily A. Dodge, born 1831.
William E. Dodge, born 1833, died 1862.
John A. Dodge, born 1834, died 1862.
Abigal M. Dodge, born 1836.

Ruth Dodge, born 1837.

Malcolm Dodge, born 1841.

Fidelia E. Dodge, born 1846.

Celeste E. Dodge, born 1848.

William Dodge, born April 20, 1813,
     Married, December 24, 1838,
Susan C. Maloney.

Samuel K. Dodge, born May 17, 1841.

Daniel Dodge, born July 11, 1843.

Cyrenius M. Dodge, born October 31, 1844.

Isabella Dodge, born February 4, 1847, died
     August 11, 1848.

Adeline Dodge, born November 17, 1849, died
     April 23, 1870.

William B. Dodge, born September 9, 1852, died
     August 11, 1854.

Charles E. Dodge, born March 12, 1855.

Buel Dodge, born August 13, 1857.

Alice A. Dodge, born April 25, 1862.

Mitchell
     Married
Emily A. Dodge.

John N. Lukins
     Married
Abigal M. Dodge, born 1836.

Amos J. Mitchell
    Married
Fidelia E. Dodge, born 1846.

R. C. Purvis
    Married
Celeste E. Dodge, born 1848.

Samuel K. Dodge, born May 17, 1841,
    Married, December 19, 1866,
Emma R. Snyder.
William L. Dodge, born June 12, 1869.
Addie Dodge, born February 15, 1874.
Florence Dodge, born March 11, 1877.
Myron S. Dodge, born April 4, 1879.

Daniel Dodge, born July 11, 1843,
    Married, June 21, 1866,
Elizabeth T. Heath, born November 6, 1846.
Blanch H. Dodge, born September 2, 1870.
Daniel H. Dodge, born December 7, 1873, died
    April 19, 1874.
Bertha M. Dodge, born February 1, 1876.
Mary Dodge, born April 28, 1878, died January
    25, 1879.
Robert G. Dodge, born May 20, 1880.

Cyrenius M. Dodge, born October 31, 1844,
    Married, March 22, 1874,
Sarah B. Cushman.
Susan F. Dodge, born June 6, 1875.
Frederick W. Dodge, born April 9, 1878.

Adam Todd Dodge, born July 23, 1792, died October 8, 1872.
        Married, November 25, 1821,
Martha King.
    Children:
Stephen A. Dodge, born September 24, 1822.
Robert King Dodge, born June 23, 1824.
Adam T. Dodge, January 30, 1826, died January 24, 1830.
Adam T. (2) Dodge, born May 5, 1830.
William H. Dodge, born July 30, 1832.
Martha E. Dodge, born November 10, 1834, died September 28, 1841.
Sarah K. Dodge, born June 18, 1837.

Stephen A. Dodge
        Married, September 12, 1844,
Elizabeth Hurley.
    Children:
Stephen A. Dodge, Jr., born July 10, 1845.
Margaret Dodge, born July 17, 1847.

Robert K. Dodge, born August 11, 1849, died
    January 25, 1852.
John K. Dodge, born August 17, 1855.
Mary E. Dodge, born April 4, 1857.

Adam T. Dodge, Jr.,
    (First) married, June 6, 1849,
Virginia Pattison. No children.
    (Second) married, May 29, 1862,
Irene E. Ayres, born May 16, 1834.
    Child:
Chauncey F. Dodge, born December 31, 1866.

William Henry Dodge, born July 30, 1832,
    Married, September 8, 1857,
Mary E. Dunn, born January 24, 1838.
    Children:
Albert W. Dodge, born September 8, 1858.
George W. Dodge, born March 8, 1860.
Henry M. Dodge, born July 29, 1866.
Elmer E. Dodge, born June 28, 1869.
Clarence B. Dodge, born March 18, 1868.

Stephen A. Dodge, Colonel of the 87th N. Y.
Volunteers, rose from the ranks to a Captaincy in
the 14th N. Y. S. M. After serving his full term in
the line, he was promoted to be Adjutant on the
staff of the late General P. S. Crooke. At the open-

ing of the war, he was advanced to "Chief of Staff," and at the end of the three months' term of the State Militia he, with the late Colonel Smith of the 13th N. Y. S. M., recruited the 87th N. Y. Volunteers in Brooklyn during the early fall of 1861.

The regiment, with Stephen A. Dodge as Colonel (Smith having been killed by a railroad accident at Plattsburgh, N. Y.), was mustered into the U. S. service, November 20, 1861, and on arrival at Washington was, at his request, transferred to the "Army of the Potomac," and assigned to Jamison's Brigade, Kearney's Division, Heinzelman's Corps, 7th Regiment. In the advance on Richmond, it shared in the siege of Yorktown; the affair at Peach Orchard; the battle of Williamsburgh; among the first to enter Fort Magruder; then at Seven Pines, and Fair Oaks, where the regiment was severely handled. Colonel Dodge fell wounded, and in the retreat was left on the field, with a Captain of the same regiment. During the night they were picked up, and cared for by General Roger A. Pryor's command of Virginia; taken to Libby Prison, and after seven or eight weeks' imprisonment, the Captain being convalescent, was sent to Andersonville Prison, and Colonel Dodge exchanged for a Colonel of a Mississippi regiment, and carried to Annapolis

Hospital. During his imprisonment and on the seven days' retreat to Harrison Landing, the 87th was greatly reduced, and the Lieutenant-Colonel taken prisoner at Second Bull Run. The regiment numbering only one hundred and thirty, it was consolidated, like numerous other decimated regiments, by order of the War Department, with the 40th N. Y. Volunteers; the Secretary of War asking the Governor of the State of New York to appoint Colonel Dodge to a new command. As he was not able then, and would not be for a year or more, to do field service, being severely wounded in the upper part of the left thigh, he was thereby compelled to resign, and received by the hand of Secretary Stanton an honorable muster out of the service.

Captain Adam Todd Dodge was a Captain in the 13th N. Y. S. M., and twice, when the regiment was called to the field, with others responded to the call, receiving favorable recognition for his promptness and loyalty, although suffering from chronic disease.

William Henry Dodge also served his term, partly in one of the New York City regiments and in the 13th N. Y. S. M.

CHAPTER VII.

CYRENIUS N. DODGE, born August 13, 1794, died
  February 14, 1863.
  Married, January 1, 1817,
Margaret Dodge, born October 23, 1787, died
  February 23, 1863.
  Children:
Sarah J. Dodge, born October 1, 1817, died June
  16, 1880.
Margaret M. Dodge, born October 28, 1820, died
  November 11, 1820.
Margaret E. Dodge, born March 25, 1822.
William M. Dodge, born September 27, 1824.

Charles B. Knudsen, born June 22, 1812,
  Married, December 31, 1840,
Sarah J. Dodge, born October 1, 1817, died June
  16, 1880.
  Children:
Charles A. Knudsen, born June 20, 1842, died
  November 13, 1854.
Margaret D. Knudsen, born February 12, 1844.

Sarah C. Knudsen, born February 6, 1846, died
    Juiy 13, 1847.
Mary E. Knudsen, born September 2, 1849, died
    February 15, 1851.
Cyrenius Knudsen, born November 29, 1851.
William D. Knudsen, September 20, 1857.

Alanson P. Brodt, born May 4, 1835,
    Married, May 15, 1872,
Margaret D. Knudsen, born February 12, 1844.

Joseph F. Florentine, born August 28, 1818,
    Married, September 16, 1850,
Margaret E. Dodge, born March 25, 1822.
  Children :
Margaret D. Florentine, born October 31, 1851,
    died August 11, 1852.
Sarah J. Florentine, born July 27, 1854.
William D. Florentine, born January 30, 1853.
Phebe M. Florentine, born February 4, 1856.
Mary Emma Florentine, born July 20, 1857.
Joseph F. Florentine, Jr., born October 24, 1859.

William D. Florentine
    Married, November 10, 1874,
Annie E. Lemon.

Child :

William J. Florentine, born August 16, 1875.

Samuel W. Raimer,   died October 8, 1879.
    Married, October 31, 1877,
Mary Emma Florentine.   No children.

William M. Dodge, born September 27, 1824,
    (1st) Married, September 6, 1848,
Susan M. Hopkins, born February 23, 1825, died
    August 7, 1853.
Child :

Edward Sanderson Dodge, born July 27, 1853,
    died January 12, 1854.

    (2d) Married, February 11, 1857,
Emma W. Sowers, born January 8, 1836, died
    July 29, 1864.
Children :

Mary S. Dodge, born November 1, 1857.
Margaret S. Dodge, born February 6, 1859.
Emma K. Dodge, born June 8, 1860.

    (3d) Married, May 16, 1866,
Mary L. Selfwich.
Children :

William L. Dodge, born March 9, 1867.
Annie L. Dodge, born May 15, 1870.
Robert E. Lee Dodge, born September 29, 1872.

Jeremiah Dodge (2), born October 15, 1755, died
    September 24, 1813.

(4th) Married
Sarah Frost, born February 26, 1762, died Novem-
    ber 29, 1824.
    Children :
John Dodge, born May 18, 1779, died December
    6, 1831.
Jeremiah Dodge (3), born July 23, 1781, died
    January 11, 1860.
Samuel Dodge.
Margaret Dodge.

John Dodge, born May 18, 1779, died December
    6, 1831.
            Married, August 16, 1804,
Jane Evans, born March, 1785, died November 20,
    1860.
    Children :
Sarah Dodge, born July 1, 1806.
Elinor M. Dodge, born July 5, 1808, died Novem-
    ber 20, 1862.
Titus E. Dodge, born June 25, 1810.
John Dodge, born September 26, 1812, died
    August 3, 1814.
Jane Dodge, born January 23, 1815.

Abraham L. Boyer, born October 4, 1803, died
    August 24, 1880.
        Married, May 9, 1829,
Sarah Dodge, born July 1, 1806.
    Children :
Mary J. Boyer,
Samuel D. Boyer,
Abraham Boyer,
William H. Boyer,
William L. Boyer,
Elinor H. Boyer,
Mary L. Boyer,
Daniel Boyer,
Hattie Boyer.

Oliver P. Hicks, died April 28, 1857,
        Married, December 21, 1842,
Elinor M. Dodge, born July 5, 1808, died Novem-
    ber 20, 1862.
    Child :
Oliver P. Hicks, Jr., born 1846.

Titus E. Dodge, born June 25, 1810,
        Married, August 17, 1831,
Mary Cumberson, born July 28, 1808, died
    Children :
Jane Dodge, born July 4, 1832, died May 5, 1849.

John L. Dodge, born February 12, 1835.

William E. Dodge, born June 14, 1837, died November 6, 1839.

Margaret Dodge, born September 15, 1840.

Mary E. Dodge, born February 4, 1843, died August 12, 1867.

William C. Dodge, born November 21, 1844, died March 2, 1847.

Sarah Dodge, born August 29, 1847, died September 4, 1848.

Sophia B. Dodge, born February 9, 1849.

Henry P. Dodge, born December —, 1855, died February 22, 1856.

William Salt
    Married, May 13, 1835,
Jane Dodge, born January 23, 1815.
    Children:
William Salt,
John Salt,
Phebe J. Salt,
Elinor Salt,
Wellington Salt,
Caroline Salt,
Mary Salt,
Daniel Salt,
Sarah Salt.

Samuel Dodge
    Married
Jane McIntyre.
    Children:
Elizabeth Dodge,
Jane Dodge,
Peter Dodge.

John L. Dodge, born February 12, 1835,
    Married
Ellen Anderson, born October 25, 1844.
    Children:
William T. Dodge, born November 25, 1864.
Edith Dodge, born April 29, 1868.
Walter Dodge, born September 19, 1876.

Geo. B. St. John
    Married
Margaret Dodge, born September 15, 1840.
No children.

Wm. H. Dermott, born January 24, 1844,
    Married, April 8, 1869,
Sophia B. Dodge, born February 9, 1849.
    Children:
Ellen Dermott, born December 21, 1870.
John T. Dermott, born January 17, 1874.
Margaret Dermott, born December 24, 1880.

Jeremiah Dodge (3), born July 23, 1781, died
   January 11, 1860.
   Married, November 16, 1805,
Eliza Brown, born April 15, 1783, died June 17,
   1860.
   Children :
Charles J. Dodge, born December 7, 1806.
Sarah A. Dodge, born August 10, 1808, died April
   16, 1877.
Jeremiah (4) Dodge, born August 30, 1810, died
   October, 1867.
William H. Dodge, born September 6, 1812.
Edward M. Dodge, born August 17, 1816, died
   November, 1874.
James P. Dodge, born October 30, 1818.
Eliza J. Dodge, born November 19, 1820, died
   December 17, 1831.
John R. Dodge, born May 30, 1823.

Charles J. Dodge, born December 7, 1806,
   Married (1st), May 31, 1825,
Maria J. Iliad, born 1808, died 1829.
   Child :
Maria E. Dodge, born June 7, 1829, died July 17,
   1830.
   Married (2d), June 14, 1832,

Mary F. Lowerree, born September 27, 1811.
Children :
Samuel W. L. Dodge, born December 8, 1833,
    died November 5, 1836.
Rebecca L. Dodge, born August 8, 1836.
Maria J. J. (wife W. L. Dubois), born June 1,
    1838.
Eliza J. Dodge, born March 29, 1839, died June
    11, 1840.
Frances O. R. Dodge, born August 8, 1841.
Robert M. G. Dodge, born July 3, 1843.
Mary L. Dodge, born July 6, 1845.
Amelia T. Dodge, born July 8, 1847.
John Ewen Dodge, born April 24, 1849.
Charlotte F. Dodge, born September 25, 1850,
    died March 6, 1852.

Frances O. R. Dodge
    Married, April 14, 1863,
Josiah P. Marquand.
Charles J. D. Marquand, born June 5, 1864, died
    June 13, 1868.
Elizabeth M. Marquand, born October 20, 1865.
Hetty W. Marquand, born July 14, 1870.
Edwin Marquand, born October 3, 1875.

Robert M. G. Dodge
    8

Married, May 23, 1865,

Lydia G. Webster, born 1846.

Stephen Webster Dodge, born June 9, 1866.

Charles J. Dodge, born June 12, 1868.

Robert M. G. Dodge, born August 18, 1871.

Amos F. H. Dodge, born July 9, 1875.

Lydia Webster Dodge, born October 5, 1879.

Amelia T. Dodge

Married, February 6, 1872,

George L. Hulin.

David Hulin, born November 6, 1872.

Alice M. Hulin, born August 18, 1876.

Caroline B. Hulin, born December 5, 1877.

Georgiana D. B. Hulin, born August 5, 1881.

John Ewen Dodge

Married, April 24, 1870,

Hannah J. Chapin.

Mary F. Dodge, born July 14, 1871.

Rebecca L. Dodge, born September 30, 1872.

Charles J. Dodge, Sr., died January 31, 1886, in his 80th year. Like his father, he was widely known and of deserved merit as ship carver in New York City, where he always resided until about twelve years before his death, when he settled at 146 Keap Street, Brooklyn, E. D.

He was for many years Colonel of the Tenth Regiment N. Y. S. M.; for over thirty years School Trustee and Commissioner; Alderman of his (11th) Ward from 1835 to 1846; prominent as a Freemason, and one of the founders and active members of the Leiderkranz Musical Society.

In all this varied and engrossing activity, he was warmly loved, honored, and lamented by a wide circle of friends, whose good esteem was his well-earned reward.

John R. Dodge, born March 18, 1824,
    Married, 1855,
Elizabeth Lawrence.
John R. Dodge, Jr.,
Charles Dodge,
Mary Dodge,
Flora P. Dodge.

Charles E. Dodge, born February 9, 1814, died
    April 18, 1876.
    Married twice. No issue.

Egbert Dodge, born October 4, 1826.
    Married, January 27, 1852,
Sarah L. Sherwood.

Children :

Thomas J. Dodge, born January 2, 1853, died September 27, 1853.

Adiel S. Dodge, born August 19, 1854.

Raymond E. Dodge, born May 10, 1856.

Emma C. Dodge, born January 25, 1858, died January 19, 1860.

Bulicka M. Dodge, born October 22, 1859, died May 26, 1864.

Ernest C. Dodge, born February 11, 1862.

Henry W. Dodge, born June 16, 1864.

David N. Dodge, born December 15, 1866.

Egbert Dodge, Jr., born January 15, 1869, died July 30, 1870.

Egbert G. Dodge, born June 1, 1873.

Wm. Halleck Dodge, born September 6, 1812, died July 29, 1838.

Married, January 30, 1832,

Mary A. Bissell, born November 25, 1809.

Children :

Jeremiah P. B. Dodge, born October 17, 1832.

Wm. H. Dodge, born October 28, 1836, died June 2, 1838.

Edwin M. Dodge, born December 1, 1838.

Jeremiah P. B. Dodge,

First, married, February 18, 1857,
Jane E. Wilson, died August 18, 1865.
  Children :
Jane E. Dodge, born December 5, 1857.
Harriet M. Dodge, died September 1, 1866.

Jeremiah P. B. Dodge,
    Second, married, October 17, 1866,
Harriet A. Wilson.
  Children :
Jeremiah V. Dodge,
Harriet A. Dodge,
Edwin V. Dodge,
Sarah A. Dodge.

Jane E. Dodge
    Married
F. C. Brown.

Edward M. Dodge, born August 17, 1816, died
    November, 1874.
    Married
Sarah A. Webb, born October 29, 1819.
  Children :
Sarah E. Dodge, born September 13, 1840, died
    March 29, 1855.
Emma L. Dodge, born September 6, 1843.

Mary J. Dodge, born December 10, 1845.

Amos C. Dodge, born March 22, 1848.

Edward M. Dodge, born August 17, 1850.

Bertram H. Dodge, born October 29, 1852.

Charlotte A. Dodge, born February 3, 1855.

Kennedy F. Dodge, born March 11, 1857.

Jerry S. Dodge, born December 29, 1858, died
    July 20, 1859.

Amelia S. Dodge, born December 29, 1858.

John F. Dodge, born June 11, 1861.

Emma L. Dodge
    Married
John W. Murray.

Mary J. Dodge
    Married
Edward P. Wilson.

CHAPTER VIII.

SAMUEL DODGE, brother of Jeremiah, first above named, and great-grandson of Tristram Dodge, the original settler (1661) of Block Island, was the second son of Samuel Dodge and his wife Elizabeth (testator in the above will probated 1766). He was born at Cow Neck, L. I., O. S. March 29, N. S. April 9, 1730; married Helena Amerman in New York, August 4, 1753 (she was born May 1, 1735, died 1817). He died at Poughkeepsie, N. Y., October 4, 1807.

He was of marked studious tastes, pursuing the science of astronomy to the close of his long life; at the age of seventy-five years he calculated with precision the coming eclipses for a century; and his elaborate work thereon, with diagrams, in his original manuscript, is still preserved; with occasional poems, that would be justly preferred to much of the domestic poetry of that early period of our literature. To the verses, of which the following is an extract, he prefaces as follows:

"In the year 1779, the author then being a member of the Legislature (of the State Assembly) from Dutchess County, New York, wrote and versified his political sentiments in the manner expressed on the succeeding pages; one of the members, having procured a copy, called one day to a number of members then in the House (the Speaker as yet not having taken the chair) to hear the political sentiments of one of their body. On reading it, some groaned and hissed, others threatened calling the author to the Bar of the House to answer for his writing such 'd——d Tory principles,' as they called them; a bystander observing that the principles of the author could not be collected from the reading; he gave it, but it would bear a *second* reading; a second reading was called for, when the reader (being instructed) read each verse; first the *former* half of each verse, and then *the latter* half of the same, *two* lines, and so on; the instability of the hearers was soon perceivable : that, by reading the same paper twice, their execrations were changed to plaudits, and the poor author came off clear."

"POLITICAL SENTIMENTS OF THE AUTHOR, 1779."

> "Hark! hark! the trumpet sounds,
> O'er seas and solid grounds,
>   The din of war's alarms,
>   Do call us all to arms.
> Who for King George do stand
>   Their honor soon will shine,
> Their ruin is at hand
>   Who with the Congress join."

Continued in this way for thirty-six lines.

The subjects of his other verses are entitled, viz.:

"The Ancient Mode of Baptism."

"On Christ's Condescension."

"On the Taking of Fort Oswego" (Lake Ontario).

"On the Taking of Fort William Henry" (Lake George).

"A Song of Praise."

"On the Fall of Minorca."

"An Acrostic Elegy on the Death of his Daughter."

———

He was keeper of the Almshouse, New York City (City Hall Park), from 1793 to 1st May, 1802. The appointment is not extant on the minutes; but on March 16, 1802, at a meeting of the Board of

Aldermen, "It was resolved that the clerk of the Board be directed to request Mr. Dodge to remove from the Almshouse (the official residence) by the first day of May next."

At the meeting of the Board of Aldermen on July 26, 1802, "An account from Mr. Dodge, formerly the keeper of the Almshouse, was received, and ordered to lie over for further consideration," and it was passed in 1803, and settled in full.

During his term of such office, on the last visit of the yellow fever to the city, he removed the inmates of the Almshouse to Poughkeepsie, where he also retired from 1802 till his death, 1807. He was active in the Revolution, Captain in New York line prior to 1779; was an original member, and signed the Institution of the Society of Cincinnati, 1783.

His sons: *Henry* Dodge was 1st Lieut. in 2d Continental (Col. Du Bois), Dutchess County; Samuel, 2d Lieut., same regiment; Richard entered—boy of thirteen years—Fifer do.

Each served till close of war.

Henry, in 1780, became Adjutant of 5th Continental, and served with Clinton's regiment in Canada.

Richard rose to Colonel's rank, and in the War of

1812 became Major-General in command of Northern frontier.

The children of the marriage of Samuel Dodge and Helen Amerman were:
(Born in New York.)

Samuel Dodge, born September 1, 1754, died October 27, 1795.

Henry Dodge, born April 12, 1756, died December 19, 1820.

William Dodge, born March 5, 1758, died 1842.

Catharine Dodge, born December 7, 1760, died November 4, 1762.

Richard Dodge, born December 31, 1762, died September 3, 1832.

Daniel Dodge, born December 14, 1764, died April 2, 1841.

Ezekiel Dodge, born February 17, 1767, died April 13, 1839.

(Born at Poughkeepsie.)

Jane Dodge, born August 15, 1769, died December 4, 1772.

James Dodge, born December 16, 1771, died October 10, 1804.

Jane Dodge (2), born December 19, 1773, died October 14, 1794.

Helena Dodge, born June 20, 1776, died September 8, 1776.

John Dodge, born December 29, 1777, died November 25, 1830.

James Dodge was a physician, and his health requiring change of air, he was appointed first in the Navy, and then U. S. Consul and Chargé d'Affaires at Tunis, Africa, in which position he rendered efficient service to many imprisoned Americans. He died at Tunis.

Samuel Dodge
   Married
Mary Forbes.
  Child :
Henry S. Dodge, born 1785, died at Brooklyn, N. Y., 1846.
   Married, 1813,
Jane Dey Varick (niece of Col. Richard Varick).
  Children :
John Varick, born 1815 (now Presbyterian minister, Evansville, Ind.).
Henry Augustus, born 1838.
Helen Kissam (wife of Judge B. S. Edwards, Springfield, Ill.).
Richard Varick (Presbyterian minister).

Henry S. Dodge, graduate of Columbia College, N. Y., was a member of the New York Bar and Master in Chancery; during the war of 1812 was Adjutant in Gen. Mapes' Brigade N. Y. S. M., and on duty at Sackett's Harbor; 1817, emigrated to Kaskaskia, Ill., returning in 1824, and died at Brooklyn, N. Y., in 1826.   His widow died in 1876, æt. 84 years.

Henry Dodge
>   Married
Sarah Rosecrans (of Verona, Oneida Co., N. Y.).
>   Children:
Harry,
James.

Catherine,
>   1st, married John Wardell.
>   2d,   "   James Wilson.
Jane
>   Married William Plummer.
Susan
>   Married Zebediah Phillips.
Eliza
William Dodge, born 1758, died 1842.
>   Children:
William Dodge,

Samuel Dodge (died single),
Helen Dodge   "   "
Eliza Dodge   "   "
John A. Dodge   "   "
Mary Dodge,
Alexander F. Dodge.

William Dodge
    Married, May 11, 1814,
Susan Johnson.
    Children :
William Dodge, born May 7, 1815, died October
    28, 1858.
Samuel Dodge, born June 21, 1818, died February
    23, 1827.
John T. Dodge, born November 3, 1816 (died
    single).
Alexander F. Dodge, born February 17, 1820.
Helen M. Dodge, born December, 1821.
Jane E. Dodge, born October 15, 1823.
Robert J. Dodge, born May 4, 1825.

Alexander F. Dodge, born about 1800,
    Married
Helen Amerman.
    Children :
Charlotte Dodge,

Elizabeth Dodge,
Mary Dodge.

Robert J. Dodge, born May 4, 1825,
     Married, June 9, 1853,
Antoinette C. Arnold, born February 23, 1836.
  Child:
Arnold R. Dodge.

William Dodge, born May 7, 1815, died October
     28, 1858.
     Married, 1851,
Mary E. Mapes.
  Children :
James M. Dodge, born June 30, 1852.
Harrington M. Dodge, born November 15, 1855,
     died 1881.

Alexander F. Dodge, born February 17, 1820,
     Married
Barbara Herwick.
  Children :
Herwick C. Dodge, May 11.
Edmund R. Dodge, February 16, 1851.
William A. Dodge,
John F. Dodge,
Ella M. Dodge,

Helen A. Dodge,
Lesley E. Dodge,
Victor E. Dodge,
Irving N. Dodge.

Charles Brombacher
Married
Charlotte Dodge.
No children.

Tracy
Married
Elizabeth Dodge.
Child:
Tracy.

Wardell,
Married
Mary Dodge.
Child:
Wardell.

Herwick C. Dodge
Married
Clara Hatfield.
Child:
Mabel C. Dodge.

Richard Dodge

> Married, 1770, February 14, New York,

Ann Sarah Irving, daughter of William and Sarah Irving, sister of Washington Irving (the author), died 1808.

Resided in Johnstown (formerly Montgomery Co.), N. Y., and died at Johnstown, N. Y., September 2, 1832.

> Children :

William Irving Dodge, born 1780, died January, 1873.

James R. Dodge, born October 27, 1795, died N. C., February 24, 1880.

Samuel Dodge, born 1798, died N. J. No issue.

Jane Ann Dodge, born January 18, 1797, married Frothingham, 1817, died at Fonda, N. Y., July, 1875.

Eliza Dodge, married Isaac Irving, April 3, 1844.

Helen Dodge, married Pierre M. Irving, 1836.

William Irving Dodge was a Captain in the war of 1812 at the battle of Plattsburgh, N. Y., marching there from Johnstown with his company, January 23, 1812. Married, at Johnstown, Patience Aiken.

9

Children :

Ann Sarah Dodge, married Henry Baldwin, February 12, 1833.

Julia Irving Dodge, married James L. Humphrey, August 12, 1842.

William James Dodge, married, Martha Humphrey, August 19, 1844.

Richard Dodge, married Elizabeth Stouts, December 4, 1849.

Elizabeth Russell Dodge.

James Richard Dodge, married, May 24, 1836, Susan Williams (N. C.).

Children:

1. Richard Irving Dodge, born at Huntsville, N. C., May 19, 1827, married (N. Y.), March 3, 1858,

Julia Rhinelander Paulding.

Children:

Frederick Paulding Dodge, born at West Point, January 29, 1859.

2. Susan Taylor, born Wilkesboro, N. C., April 20, 1859, married Frank McMillan, 30 May, 1853.   No issue.

3. Ann Sarah, born Wilkesboro, N. C., May 31, 1831, married C. L. Glinn, December 17, 1859.

4. Mary Helen, born Wilkesboro, N. C., March 15, 1835.

Richard Irving Dodge, now Colonel, U. S. A., appointed A. D. C. on staff of General Sherman, January 1, 1880; entered cadet at West Point Military Academy, July 1, 1844, graduating 1st July, 1848; was commissioned as Brevet Second Lieutenant 8th Infantry; until 1856 engaged in active duty on the South-west Frontier and New Mexico; in battle with Camanche Indians on San Saba River, Texas, March 22, 1851, and in frequent skirmishes.

September, 1854.   Adjutant 8th Infantry and First Lieutenant; 1858–1860, appointed Military Instructor Inf. tactics, West Point, and on recruiting service; 1861, Captain 8th Infantry.

1861. July 21. In battle of Bull Run, Va.

August. Defences of Washington.

September. In command Instruction Camp, Elmira, N. Y.

October. Mustering and disbursing officer, Pennsylvania and Maryland.

1862. Lieutenant-Colonel, Staff Assistant Inspector-General Fourth Army Corps.

1860. Major 12th Infantry and Assistant Prov. Marshal.

1865. Brevet Lieut.-Colonel for meritorious and faithful services in the recruitment of the armies; U. S. Asst. Prov. Marshal, New York City.

1866. Transferred to 30th Infantry on frontier service, 1867–71.

1869. Transferred to 3d Infantry. Member of Board to perfect Army Regulations, 1871–72.

1872–80. On frontier service. Lieut.-Col. 23d Infantry, October 29, 1873.

1875. In command of Exploring Expedition to Black Hills, Dak., May to October.

1876. In command of artillery and infantry of Gen. Crook's force, on winter campaign against Sioux Indians.

1878. In command of expedition against Cheyennes.

1880. In command of the infantry of Mackenzie's force in campaign against the Utes.

He is also the author of the following works, his matured observation during his extended military service on the frontier :

1. "The Plains of the Great West" (1876).
2. "The Black Hills"   do.
3. "Our Wild Indians"   (1882.)

Daniel Dodge
> Married Ann Turner, March 17, 1796, who was born New York, January 6, 1776, and died at Brooklyn, October, 1867.
> Children :

Ann Eliza Dodge, born 1801, widow of William Wheeler.

Richard J. Dodge, born 1807.

Emeline A. Dodge, born 1809.

Susan A. Dodge, born 1819, wife R. B. Despard.

Descendants (first generation) of Ezekiel Dodge, born in New York, February 17, 1767, died April 13, 1839, and Jane Power, of Poughkeepsie, born 1780, died March 15, 1837, married May 20, 1806:

> 1st. Samuel, born in New York, March 15, 1808, went away (supposed to have gone West) August 23, 1833.
> 2d. Catharine Sophia, born in Poughkeepsie, August 23, 1809.
> 3d. Mary, born in Poughkeepsie, June 1, 1811.
> 4th. Elizabeth, born in Poughkeepsie, March 29, 1813.

5th. Emily, born in New York, June 10, 1815.

6th. James Monroe, born in New York, May 11, 1817, died January 19, 1839.

7th. Augustus Power, born in New York, October 16, 1819, drowned at Sacramento, Cal., July 25, 1849.

Elizabeth Dodge, born March 29, 1813,
    Married, October 31, 1841,
William Everit.
    Children :
Elizabeth Everit, born November 29, 1842, died June 23, 1844.
William Dodge Everit, born February 4, 1844.
Augustus Dodge Everit, born December 27, 1845.
Theodore Lewis Everit, born November 11, 1847.
Eugene Everit, born June 8, 1850.
Eugenia Everit, born June 8, 1850, died November 16, 1851.
Edward Everit, born January 20, 1854, died September 17, 1854.

Eugene Everit
    Married, May 27, 1880,
Delmere W. Merritt.
    Children :
Eugenie Everit, born March, 1881.

John Dodge, born 1777, died November 25, 1830,
   Married at New York, April 9, 1801,
Margaret E. Wood.
   Children :
John W. Dodge, born November 4, 1807.
Matilda Dodge, wife William Tracy.
Clarissa Dodge, wife Marschalk.
Charlotte Dodge, wife Henry O. Wardell.
Catharine Clay Dodge, wife William P. Coles.
James Lawrence Dodge.
Edward Samuel Dodge.
Richard Montgomery Dodge.
Stephen Clay Dodge.
Amelia Dodge.
William Henry.

John W. Dodge was elected Associate of N. Academy of Design in 1832. Settled in Chicago, Ill., as Vice-President of Chicago Academy. Celebrated artist in portraits and miniatures. Those of President Jackson, Henry Clay, Henry Bergh, and others are widely known and esteemed.

CHAPTER IX.

As before stated, Israel Dodge, one of the sons of Tristram Dodge (senior), early emigrated from Block Island, and settled at New London, in the Colony of Connecticut.

Among the new inhabitants, between 1670 and 1700, recorded in "Calkins' History of New London," is Israel Dodge, as purchasing and settling on a considerable farm in the North Parish of New London in 1694, which was forty-eight years after the first effort to create the settlement of the town in 1646.

In 1705, at the session of the Queen's (Anne) Court Commission, among those returned as settled on Indian lands is Israel Dodge. This same tract of land—now Montville—is yet vested in his descendants.

The first record of freemen of New Shoreham, Block Island, as we have seen, was in 1670, and contained his name.

He may, then, have been *born* about 1649 in England.

The records of the Town Clerk of New London, prior to 1781, were destroyed, with other valuable papers, by the burning of the town, its court house, and most of its dwellings, in the barbarous raid of Benedict Arnold, September 6, 1781 ; but a portion of the Probate Records and Registry of early Deeds escaped.

Among these we find his will, proved 1745; which being taken as the year of his death, gives him the advanced age of ninety-six years.

Israel Dodge (Junior), his son, had, in 1743, enlisted for the " French War," in the contingent of Colonial Troops that served on the expedition against Cape Breton ; and in the next spring (1744) is returned as having died in camp from fever.

John Dodge, another son, born at New London in 1727, and died in Connecticut, 1792 ; married, October 23, 1748, Lydia Rogers, of Pomfret, Conn.

They had the family, viz.:

Jordan Dodge, born August 6, 1749.

John Dodge, born July 12, 1751.

Peter Dodge, born November 17, 1753, died 1759.

Israel Dodge, born September 3, 1760.

Josiah Rogers Dodge, born September 28, 1762.

Jeriel Dodge, born September 28, 1768, died 1770.

Christopher Dodge, born July 6, 1765.

Nehemiah Dodge, born July 3, 1770.

Elizabeth Dodge, born November 7, 1750.

Lydia Dodge, born May 8, 1758.

Among whom, we find Rev. Nehemiah Dodge, prominent as pastor of the First Baptist Church at New London; and from 1823 pastor of the First Universalist Society there, and afterwards in New York City. From him descend the following well-known citizens, some of eminence in their profession :

Rev. Nehemiah Dodge died at New London, Conn., June 4, 1843,
> Married

Lucy Smith, of Lynn, Conn. (who died September 25, 1868).
> Children :

Nehemiah Dodge.

Joseph Smith (M. D.), of New York, born at Lebanon, Conn., August 23, 1806.

Mary Ann, wife of John Woodward.

(Dr.) Joseph Smith Dodge
> (1st) Married, October 14, 1828,

Julia A. Burgess.

Children:

Julia A. Dodge, 1829–33.

Harriet J. Dodge, October 17, 1831, wife (1854) of W. C. Horne, of Florence, Italy.

Joseph Smith, Jr., December 3, 1834,
    Married
Mary R. Hall (of Stamford, Conn.).
(Children: Arthur, Julia, Walter, Alice, Herman Dodge.)
Julia E., March 19, 1843.

Henry Nehemiah, May 19, 1843,
    Married
Mary L. Danforth, of Morristown, N. J.
(Children: Ruth P., Edith, Mary Dodge.)
Lucy Emma, wife of W. A. Buckmaster, Esq.

Dr. Joseph S. Dodge
    Married (2d), April 22, 1852,
Alania Burger.
    Children:
Ella, born November 18, 1854.
Amy L., born February 3, 1857.
Samuel W., born 1859.

Of the family of John and Lydia Dodge (Rogers), their son *Israel*, third of the name in his line, true

to the adventurous spirit of his ancestors, left home
when only fifteen years old, and made several
voyages to the African coast. At eighteen he
enlisted in the Revolutionary army, and at the
Battle of Brandywine (September 11, 1777) was
wounded by a bayonet charge of the British line.
In 1782, Virginia, claiming title to the disputed
Mississippi Valley, by commission of Patrick Henry,
Governor, appointed his brother, Col. John Dodge,
to command the Illinois country. Israel became
Lieutenant under him, and was stationed at Kaskaskia. He had shortly before, at Carlisle, Pa., married Anne (Nancy) Hunter. On a journey, with his
wife, to Bairdstown, Ky., they halted at the French
Post of Vincennes, where their son Henry was born
on October 12, 1782. He built the first stone house
at Bairdstown, now Kentucky.

Attracted by the large grants of land offered by
the King of Spain to all who would settle in his
Colony, which then included the whole region south
of the Ohio River and west of the Alleghany
Mountains southward to the Gulf of Mexico, Israel
Dodge mounted his horse, and, riding over what became the Territories of Indiana and Illinois, crossed
the "Father of Waters" to the ancient town of St.
Genevieve, now in Missouri. Here he erected mills

and made other public improvements, for which he received large grants of land from His Catholic Majesty. In descending the Mississippi River with products of his farm and mills, he was captured by pirates, who subsequently released him, with his crew and cargo, for a small ransom, paid in pork and flour. New Orleans then belonged to Spain, and pirates and robbers infested the land, but they did not prevent Israel Dodge from his extended journeys. It was on one of those saddle-rides, from Bairdstown to St. Genevieve, by land, that his oldest son, Henry, was born at the French Post Vincennes, on the Wabash; his parents being detained at that post, in consequence of high waters on the river. Henry was so named for a gunsmith (Moses Henry), who saved the life of the infant boy when but a few weeks old, and in the grasp of a savage, who was on the eve of dashing out his brains. Israel Dodge was appointed the first High Sheriff, in 1804, of St. Genevieve County, by Gen. Wilkinson, President Jefferson's Military Governor, who took possession of Upper Louisiana under the Treaty of 1803. His active and adventurous life early terminated in his forty-sixth year. Among his pleasant recollections was to have witnessed the hauling down of the white flag of France, surrendering all design of

colonization in America, and the hoisting of the
Star Spangled Banner, March 30, 1804. This cere-
monial was performed by Major Stoddard, of our
Army, and the Baron de Carondelet ; amid the tears
and lamentations of the French, who were sincerely
attached to their old government, and the shouts
and plaudits of the few Americans present.

His son, the Hon. Henry Dodge, was born in
1782 ; fitly beginning in the wilderness a life which,
above all others of the North-west, was destined to
be that of their bravest and wisest leader, in their
rapid growth to dominant power. His father had
settled in Missouri, then a Spanish possession, at
the village of St. Genevieve, on the River Mississippi, in the County of St. Genevieve, where he
lived till his death in 1806.

REMINISCENCES BY GENERAL A. C. DODGE.

[From his Address before the Old Settlers of Clark County, Mo., in the Fall
of 1883.]

More than fifteen years before the star of empire passed from
Napoleon to Jefferson, my grandparents, paternal and maternal,
migrated from Kentucky to the then Spanish province of Upper
Louisiana. The Dodges located in St. Genevieve County, the
McDonalds near St. Louis. They were tempted thither by re-

ports of the rich lands and lead mines which were offered without price to all who would occupy and improve them. My grandfather, Israel Dodge, settled at New Bourbon, near the goodly old French town St. Genevieve, where his ashes repose. For improvements, such as the cultivation of the soil, building mills and distilleries (the King of Spain was not a prohibitionist), he received large grants of land. Surrounded by savages, and remote from market, such grants were comparatively of small value. Strange to say, however, long years after the title had passed from his descendants, one of these tracts of land, otherwise poor, thus granted to Israel Dodge, furnished the matchless stone used in the erection of the magnificent Capitol at Des Moines. A Connecticut Yankee, full of the enterprise that belonged to his race, Israel Dodge constructed the rude craft known as the "flat-bottomed boat," the "old broad scow," and shipped the products of his farm and mills to New Orleans, then a Spanish town. An incident of one of his voyages illustrates the perils which beset life and property in those days. When far down on the Lower Mississippi, his boat was boarded in broad daylight by a modern "Rob Roy," with a band of river pirates, who, placing their guns at the heads of my grandfather and his crew, ordered them to row ashore, that they might appropriate the cargo to their own use. A second lieutenant in the Revolutionary war, wounded by a British bayonet at Brandywine, Israel Dodge's familiarity with danger and death enabled him to retain his self-possession. Noticing something in the bearing or language of the pirate chief which induced the belief that he was a Mason, he gave him a sign or grip, whereof I am ignorant, not being of the initiated. This brought the exclamation from the man of robbery and blood, "Boys! we must let this man and his boat go!" They did so, the chief graciously accepting a barrel of flour and some bacon as a present. Rejoicing at the fortunate escape, my grandfather proceeded on to New Orleans, sold

his cargo at high prices, was paid in good money, Spanish gold,
and returned home in safety with his companions. In the " Bon
Homme " (Good Man's) settlement, a few miles west of St. Louis, in
the year 1800, the father of the speaker led his mother to the hyme-
neal altar, the high contracting parties having attained the respective
ages of nineteen and fifteen. Thirty-seven years later the speaker
journeyed from Wisconsin to Missouri, to perform a like act of civil-
ity for a lady who had been his schoolmate, her father being their
teacher, and whom he was so fortunate as to woo and win in their
native county (St. Genevieve). With abundant opportunities of
knowing, he was ready to certify, in or out of court, that no State
could furnish better wives than Missouri. The speaker then went on
to say that as a friend to matrimony and to early marriages, he suggested that these old settlers' reunions, so largely attended by the
young people of both sexes, afforded admirable opportunities for
young people to do a little innocent courting, and he would advise
every faint-hearted swain present to pluck up courage and to " pop
the question " to the girl of his choice, and thus end one of the great
events of human life. The occasion is joyous and the surroundings
are favorable to the success of his venture. Milton says :

> " Of earthly good, the best is a good wife."

> —*Burlington Evening Post,* Aug. 2, 1884.

Unconsciously, while he journeyed, through the
necessities of European wars and cabinets, the
political and national firmament were beginning to
change, and a new and wider horizon was opening
to a boundless future of growth and power.

By treaty of 1800, the whole region south of the

Ohio, or the great valley of the Mississippi to the Gulf of Mexico, with undefined western bounds, was ceded by Spain to the French Republic. Our sagacious Jefferson, by his special envoy, Monroe, found the First Consul Napoleon, in 1803, ready to cede, for fifteen millions of dollars, *all* this vast *region*.

The area was greatly beyond his first intentions, which were limited to New Orleans, the river and its valley. Missouri, and all the wide West (*perhaps California*) and the South-west, were included in the "Louisiana purchase," so called, and ceded by Napoleon through the Treaty of 30th April, 1803.

Henry Dodge, son of the last-named Israel, was born October 12, 1782, at the well-known French village or "Post Vincennes," on the Wabash River, now in the State of Indiana ; his parents being *en route* from what is now Kentucky to Missouri, both places being then in the Spanish province of Upper Louisiana. He was educated in a log school-house at Bairdstown, Kentucky. Of his school-mates, older than he, we may mention Felix Grundy, John Rowan, and John Pope, of Kentucky ; distinguished as Senators and Jurists. He afterwards read law for some two years in the office of the brave but unfortunate Colonel Allen, who fell in the war

10

of 1812, at the disastrous battle on the River
Raisin. Of his uncles, on the maternal and paternal side, six had fallen under the murderous Indian
hatchet.

Among his very earliest recollections was to
have seen the dead and mangled body of one of
those uncles brought to the rude stockade or " Fort
Vincennes " in the arms of another uncle on horseback. At the age of twenty-one he became High
Sheriff of St. Genevieve County, Missouri, thus filling the place to which his father had been appointed
by General Wilkinson, who, when both were under
age, had served with his father in the war of the
Revolution.

Henry Dodge was naturally a leader of his fellow-
men. Commencing as a subaltern, and filling every
intermediate rank, he was appointed a Brigadier-
General of Missouri Volunteers by President Madison, in 1814; and afterwards, under the State
organization, was unanimously elected Major-
General.

At the commencement of the war of 1812, he was
first called by General Howard, then Governor of
Missouri, to defend the exposed frontiers, which he
did successfully at the head of two mounted regiments. He coöperated by land with Major, after-

wards President, Zachary Taylor, who commanded
some twenty-two gun-boats against the Indians, then
led by their celebrated chief, "Black Partridge."
The array of the forces thus led by land and water
alarmed the Indians, who retreated to Fort Clark
(Peoria), their place of rendezvous. Referring to
this expedition, Wetmore, in his *Gazetteer* of Missouri, says:

"After two years of hard fighting 'on their own
hook,' the Booneslick settlement made application
to Governor Clark for aid; and a detachment of
Rangers, under the command of General Dodge,
was sent to their relief. It is reported of this officer,
that when his line of march was obstructed by the
Missouri, on his route to the Miami village, he
dashed into the river, followed by the Rangers, sitting steady and erect in their saddles, who swam
their horses to the opposite shore. The transit of
their ammunition had been secured in a canoe. By
this accelerated movement the Miamis were sur-
prised and captured in their village."

The Indians, by flight, evaded a general engage-
ment; and when he reached the village, they surrendered and asked that their lives might be spared.
It was only, however, by throwing himself between
the Indians and the guns of a portion of his com-

mand (the "Booneslickers" so-called); that he was
able to save from indiscriminate slaughter some
four hundred and eighty men, women, and children
of the Miami tribe, and that, too, after they had
surrendered and given up their arms.

In 1820 he was elected a member of the convention to form a constitution for the State of Missouri,
and also appointed United States Marshal. He
filled the latter place until he left the State. Among
the pleasing incidents of his life was the heartfelt
gratification afforded him, in his capacity of Major-
General, to receive and do honor to the Marquis de
La Fayette, when, in 1825, that great and good man
visited Missouri.

In 1827, upon the discovery of lead ore at the
"Upper Mississippi Mines" (in Northern Illinois and
Michigan Territory), now Wisconsin, he migrated
thither; those mines having awakened an excite-
ment in the Western Country second only to that
caused later by the discovery of gold in California.

Simultaneously with his arrival, the Winnebago
tribe of Indians had raised the tomahawk, and
were killing and scalping men, women, and children,
and also attacking the "keel boats" then engaged
in conveying supplies to the miners. Without organization, and with but few arms, the people,

driven into what is now Galena, Illinois, upon " the flat," in front of that town, unanimously elected General Dodge to chief command. With character- istic energy, he caused block-houses to be erected throughout the mining country, and spikes to be manufactured and attached to the ends of long poles for defence of the stockade " Forts," to which the people fled for protection. But prone rather to give than to receive blows, he led a small mounted force, all that could be raised, to the Indian towns on the Pecatonica and the Wisconsin rivers; swim- ing the last-named river four times in pursuit of the enemy. The murderers were surrendered by their tribe; tried, convicted, and pardoned by John Quincy Adams, then President.

" Grim-visaged war having for a time smoothed his wrinkled front," with other pioneers, General Dodge moved into the Indian country, discovered valuable mines, and settled the place called in his honor, *Dodgeville*, the present seat of justice for Iowa County, Wis. Here he pursued for several years, with his usual energy, the business of mining and smelting lead ore. He was among the first who erected the rude furnace of that day, for the manu- facture of lead, within that territory (then Michi- gan). From a point high up on the Wisconsin

River, in the frail "flat-bottomed boat," so called,
he shipped quantities of lead to New Orleans, a
distance of more than 1,500 miles. Other persons
engaged in the same business reshipped their car-
goes at St. Louis; placing them on board elegant
steamers, while he made the entire voyage to New
Orleans in the same frail and primitive craft. It
was an enterprise of great peril and hardship, requiring some three months for its performance.

In 1829, at the first organization of Iowa County,
Wis., he was elected, on the same day, Chief-Justice
of the County and Colonel of its militia. In the
former capacity, with two associates, William Schuyler Hamilton, third son of General Alexander Hamilton (of New York), and James H. Gentry, as
colleagues, he held the first court in Iowa County.
It was as Colonel of *Michigan* Volunteers, bearing
the commission of the late Lewis Cass, as Governor
of the Territory, that he won his laurels in the contest against " Black Hawk."

1832. In this year, and in the month of April,
the evil genius of that renowned chieftain led him
to cross the " Father of Waters " in hostile array,
and without provocation, to invade Illinois and
Wisconsin. To General Dodge it immediately
became apparent that the people in the " Lead

Mines" were in great peril, and that their country must soon become the theater of bloody war. Early in the month of May he called for volunteers, and at the head of a small force, among whom, it may be mentioned, were his two sons and a son-in-law, Paschal Beguette; he marched in the direction of what is now Dixon, Ill., to watch the movements of the Indians, and to learn whether the affair would end in war or peace.   In the previous year (1831), the philanthropic General Gaines had bought peace from treacherous Black Hawk and his followers by giving them 10,000 bushels of corn, and also several thousand dollars' worth of presents, upon their solemn treaty stipulation never again to come east of the Mississippi River.

The expedition of General Dodge was timely, and proved his sagacity.   For, on the 14th day of May, Major Stillman, at the head of some three hundred Illinois Volunteers, was signally defeated by Black Hawk; who killed and scalped a number of Stillman's men, chasing the main body some thirty miles, under the sound of the war-whoop.   This flight inaugurated savage warfare.   It was soon followed by murders in every direction; by the successive defeats of Captain A. W. Snyder, Colonel James W. Stevenson, and Major John Dement, all belonging to the Illinois Volunteers, and officers of high character and well-known courage.

Throughout the valley of the Rock River the war was fierce and unremitting, and the tomahawk bathed in gore. The farmer reaped his harvest in the dress and with the arms of the volunteer, and often left his plough to join in the tumult of battle or share the dangers of pursuit. General Dodge posted his small force in advance of the settlements, and, by sagacious leadership, triumphed over the treacherous savages, inflicting great injury upon them, with slight loss to his command.

In brief, the main events of this campaign, which lasted from spring to autumn, 1832, were his expeditions to Dixon, Ill., and to Ottawa ; his conference at the "Four Lakes" with the Chief "Spotted Arm" and his band, intended to prevent the Winnebagoes from uniting their forces with those of "Black Hawk"; his seizure of Indian spies at the Blue Mound, thus thwarting their purpose ; his eloquent address to the volunteers at "Kirker's Grove," and his successful plan for the recovery of two young ladies—the Misses Hall—captives of the savages, after the murder of their parents and entire family, with numerous other expeditions for the protection of his fellow-citizens. His battle of the Pecatonica, fought on the 6th of June, 1832, at the " Horse Shoe Bend " on that stream, though small in numbers engaged, will ever be regarded as one of the most desperate engagements in the history of Indian warfare. Senator McRoberts, of Illinois, referring to this fight (see Appendix to *Congressional Globe*, 27th Congress, 1st session, page 101), said: " Dodge and his party pursued and overtook them. The enemy, finding they could not make their escape, posted themselves for battle. Now, here was just the situation to test the courage and devotion of any man to his country. The exasperated enemy were armed with the rifle, tomahawk, and spear, and accustomed all their lives to the use of these weapons. The Indians had a decided advantage in position, protected by an embankment and the trees of the forest ; they had also the first fire. To dislodge them, a charge must be made over the open prairie, in the most exposed of all possible situations, and, from the number and desperation of the enemy, at great sacrifice of human life. In such a position, what is the course of Dodge and his brave associates ? They resolved to dislodge the enemy, or perish in the attempt. They dismount from their horses, and, headed by their commander, charge the enemy on foot. They receive his fire

when almost at the muzzle of the guns; a desperate
conflict ensues between the survivors and the
enemy. After each party had delivered its fire, it
became a personal encounter between exasperated
combatants. The enemy all fell; eighteen Indians
were killed, and four whites; Dodge had but
twenty-one men. I met him and the survivors of
his party a few days afterward, and some of them
still carried on their persons the evidence of the
conflict, and their clothes were burnt with powder."

He also led the advance at the battles of Wisconsin Heights and Bad Axe.

Although these combats, if measured by the
numbers engaged on his side, would seem small in
contrast with modern wars, yet, in fact, they were
triumphs of skill and courage. With a small force,
unsupported by any large reserve, unaided; he met
and conquered numbers of the most sagacious, wily,
and sanguinary of the Indian race, aiding in subdu-
ing them, and bringing their Chief, Black Hawk,
and his leading braves into captivity.

1833. Upon the termination of the campaign
against Black Hawk, Colonel Dodge was appointed
by President Jackson to the command of a battal-
ion, consisting of 1,000 mounted Rangers, raised by

Act of Congress for the protection of the frontier. At the end of a year's service in command of the Rangers, he was called to the command of the first regiment of Dragoons ever enlisted in the Army of the United States.   Of this regiment, S. W. Kearney and R. B. Mason were respectively Lieutenant-Colonel and Major, and Jefferson Davis, late President of the Confederacy, Adjutant.

1834. He moved from Fort Gibson, Arkansas, with 500 Dragoons, in the direction of the headwaters of the Arkansas River, to reclaim prisoners in captivity in the villages of the Camanche, Kioway, and other hostile tribes.   General Leavenworth, of the United States Army, started in command of the expedition, and, with five other officers, died on the route, leaving the chief command to devolve on Colonel Dodge.   The Indians surrendered when he reached their towns, delivering over the prisoners ; making the expedition a success, but at severe loss, for, besides above six officers, eighty dragoons perished on the march.

The Secretary of War (Cass), in his report of 1834, speaks in high terms of the "valuable service rendered by Colonel Dodge and his command on that trying expedition."

In 1835 he marched from Fort Leavenworth, on

the Missouri, up the Platte River far into the
Rocky Mountain region—then almost a Terra In-
cognita—visiting some thirty or more tribes, with
whom he formed treaties of amity. On his return,
Congress published a thousand copies of his Journal, and General Gaines, commanding the Western
Department of the Army, recommended that a
sword should be presented to Colonel Dodge, and
that his officers and men should receive a month's
extra pay. Hon. William Medill, Governor and
member of Congress from Ohio, referring to this
expedition (see Appendix to *Cong. Globe*, page
280, 27th Congress, 2d session), said:

"In conclusion, Mr. Chairman, let us turn from
this humiliating picture of human nature, and
inquire for a moment who it was that was *removed*
to make room for this man. When the Western
frontiers were invaded by the savage hordes of the
wilderness, and the progress of civilization retarded
for a time by the tomahawk and scalping-knife, who
was it that exposed his life and endured the most
extraordinary hardships in defending the home and
fireside of the emigrant? Who was it that met in
mortal combat, and arrested the career of the murderous, but brave and intrepid, Black Hawk; and

first caused the sound of our cannon to be heard on the other side of the Rocky Mountains? Who commanded the Volunteers at the memorable battle of Wisconsin Heights, where, sustained on either side by one of his own youthful but gallant sons, he occupied the post of danger, and vanquished a superior foe, with the loss of but a single man? Who led on the charge at Bad Axe, and shed such lustre upon the valor of his countrymen at Pecatonica, where not a solitary man of the enemy survived to relate the incidents of the fatal conflict? The name of *General Dodge is identified with the history and glory of the West, and will ever be held in grateful remembrance by a people whom his chivalry and valor have delivered from cruelty and death.* Selected for that purpose by President Jackson, he explored the vast regions of wilderness on this side of Oregon; at the head of his invincible dragoons visited and entered into treaties of amity with numerous tribes of Indians hitherto unknown, released the whites that were found in captivity, and restored peace, order, and quietude upon the whole line of the frontier. His extraordinary services and signal success drew from General Gaines, the commander of the Division, a letter recommending him to the notice of Congress, and

suggested that a sword be presented him, as a token
of national gratitude.   Honored and esteemed by
the people, though proscribed by the President
(John Tyler), he was chosen by the citizens of
Wisconsin to represent their interest upon this
floor, where he has again had the pleasure of meeting one of those sons who fought by his side at
Wisconsin Heights, and who has been honored with
a similar trust from the Territory of Iowa.   Such is
an example of the 'reform' which is practiced by
this Administration."

1836, July 4. When not a hostile Indian was to
be found in the North or South-west, and tribes
recently the terror of the frontier were glad to
remain in peace at their old homes, or be transported to new lands beyond the great River
Missouri; President Jackson called General Dodge
from the command of his Dragoons, to be Governor
and Superintendent of Indian Affairs for the new
Territory of Wisconsin; larger much in extent than
the Empire of France under the first Napoleon. It
comprised the present States of Wisconsin, Iowa,
Minnesota, and about half of Dakota Territory.
It had then one delegate to Congress, and less than
twenty-three thousand inhabitants.   Now the same

country has six (6) Senators, with twenty-five (25) Representatives in Congress; and a larger population than the United States contained in 1812, during their second war against Great Britain.

In its earliest history, Wisconsin belonged to France and England. But, at the termination of the War of the Revolution, by the definitive treaty of peace, September 3, 1783, Virginia, aided by the genius of Patrick Henry (then her Governor), and by the valor of her troops, led by the heroic George Rogers Clark—having conquered and brought within her chartered limits the region now embraced in Ohio, Indiana, Illinois, Michigan, Wisconsin, and about half of Minnesota; with a generosity characteristic of that great Commonwealth, the mother of States and statesmen—voluntarily ceded to the United States all claim to this great North-west Territory. Her deed of cession, executed March 1, 1784, bears the honored names of Thomas Jefferson and James Monroe. In 1787, by the memorable ordinance of the Continental Congress, the North-west Territory was organized over this vast region.

From 1789 to 1800 Wisconsin formed a part of the Territory of Ohio; from 1800 to 1809, of Indiana; from 1809 to 1818, of Illinois; from 1818 to 1836, a part of Michigan.

Upon Governor Dodge devolved the delicate and important duty, of putting into operation the machinery of government over this vast Territory of Wisconsin. All the officers, civil and military, were to be appointed ; the census to be taken; members of the two houses of Assembly to be apportioned among the different counties; and the Legislature to be convened at such place as the Governor might designate. He was, moreover, in that year appointed Commissioner to hold treaty conferences; one with the Menominee tribe, at Green Bay, and the other at the present site of Davenport, Iowa. To both places, as to all others visited, he rode on horseback. These duties he performed successfully ; extinguishing the Indian title to large bodies of land on both sides of the Mississippi, and meeting the Legislature, October 25, 1836, at Belmont, Iowa County (now La Fayette, Wis.). At this session, the capital was located permanently at the beautiful site of *Madison;* where it still remains, and temporarily at Burlington, now in Iowa, where it continued until July 4, 1838, when the Territories were divided.

In 1837 he negotiated treaties with the Chippewa and other Indian tribes; for the vast district of pine lands lying upon the Chippewa, Black, St. Croix, and other rivers of Wisconsin and Minnesota. No measure, perhaps, ever contributed so much to the development and rapid settlement of the North-west. Anterior to that date, all the pine lumber used in many of the Western States and Territories was transported, at enormous cost, thousands of miles down the Ohio and up the Mississippi rivers.

Clothed with the power of appointing all officers, civil and military ; with an absolute veto upon the acts of the General Assembly ; and unrestricted par-doning power ; his administration was, nevertheless, so acceptable to the governed, that, yielding to the expressed wishes of the General Assembly and the people, without distinction of party, he was re-ap-pointed by President Van Buren in 1839.

Upon the advent, however, of the Whig Party to power, in 1841, he was, from political considerations, removed ; and the Hon. James D. Doty and, after him, ex-Senator Nathaniel P. Talmadge, of New York, appointed his suceessors, and they served during the administration of President Tyler.

The " proscribed of the President became the choice of the people." Immediately upon his removal, in 1841, Governor Dodge was nominated by the Democratic Party, to whose principles and organization he was ever faithful, and elected to

II

Congress by an overwhelming majority over his Whig competitor, the Hon. J. E. Arnold, a much respected and talented member of the Milwaukee Bar. On their meeting after the election, Mr. Arnold jocosely remarked: " Why, Governor, our race was like that of a colt contending against a veteran war-horse."

By all the ties that bind man to his fellow-men, Henry Dodge was the friend of the hardy and deserving pioneer; by whom he was equally cherished and revered. In his second message, delivered at Burlington in November, 1837, among other things in favor of pre-emptions, graduation of price, and homesteads, he said : " Land is the immediate gift from God to man, and should not be used by our Government for speculation, etc." He was also a warm supporter of appropriations for rivers and harbors; and had the gratification to obtain the appropriation for the harbor at Milwaukee and other points upon the western shore of Lake Michigan. He spoke but seldom, and generally for measures of interest to his constituents or defense of the frontier. His speech (never reported at any length) in favor of remounting the 2d Regiment of Dragoons, triumphantly carried the measure, and was admired by all, drawing from John Quincy

Adams, who followed in the debate, a handsome compliment, Adams referring to him as "the eloquent delegate from Wisconsin."

In 1843, Governor Dodge was again returned to Congress, beating his worthy neighbor, General Hicox, by a larger majority than that by which he had triumphed over Arnold.

In 1845, at the conclusion of his four years' service in the House of Representatives, he was recalled by President Polk to his old place as Governor of Wisconsin, in deference to the voice of the people, in which capacity he continued to serve until her admission as a State, May 29, 1848.

At the meeting of the first Legislature, in June of the last-named year, there was an animated and bitter contest for senatorial honors among the leading politicians of the State. Governor Dodge was chosen over distinguished competitors, such as Chief-Justice Dunn, Governor Doty, and other aspirants. In the classification precedent to the admission of the first Senators from a new State, he drew the term of four years, and was re-elected, in 1852, by a much larger majority, for a full term, which expired the 4th of March, 1857.

In 1844, with a degree of self-abnegation and modesty peculiar to him, he *refused* to answer a letter written by the late Hon. Robert Dale Owen, of Indiana, a greatly esteemed friend and representative from his native State, and signed by some five or six members of the House of Representatives, asking his views upon the Texas, Oregon, Tariff, and other public questions; the object of the letter being to bring Governor Dodge prominently before the Democratic Presidential Convention of that year, which nominated Mr. Polk.

Although his opinions upon all of these questions were in full harmony with those of the requisite two-thirds majority in the convention of his party, he refused the use of his name to beat his valued personal and political friend, Martin Van Buren, whose defeat in 1840 he thought ought to be righted by a triumph in 1844.

In 1848, just after he had taken his seat in the Senate, he was unanimously nominated by the Democratic Convention, held at Utica, N. Y., for Vice-President of the United States, to run upon the same ticket with his old friend, Ex-President Van Buren. He, however, promptly declined the honor, which was subsequently bestowed, by the Buffalo Convention, upon Charles Francis Adams.

At the termination of his senatorial career, he declined the office of Governor of Washington Territory, tendered to him by President Pierce, with a fixed determination never again to accept public station.

As a tribute to his worth, the Legislature of Wisconsin passed an Act "to perpetuate the memory of the late Governor Dodge," directing that his bust, in marble, be placed within the Capitol of the State. It stands there, in Italian marble, an excellent likeness of the venerable patriot and statesman, the brave soldier and honest man, who was gathered to his fathers on the 19th day of June, 1867, at the house of his only surviving son, in Burlington, Iowa. He was the great and successful captain of the civilization of Wisconsin.

Of singularly commanding person, he was six feet in height, perfectly erect, and possessing a herculean constitution; he was rigidly temperate and abstemious throughout his long life. He was fond of reading the Scriptures, especially "Scott's Bible" and its notes. In the latter part of his life he was a regular attendant upon divine service, and some years before his death joined the Episcopal Church at Mineral Point, Wisconsin.

The following eloquent and truthful tribute is from the pen of Governor Fairchild, on the occasion of the death of Henry Dodge:

(From the Madison Journal).

" The late ex-Governor and ex-Senator Dodge :

" Governor Fairchild, of Wisconsin, has issued the following executive order on the death of Hon. Henry Dodge, formerly Governor of Wisconsin :

" MADISON, WIS., *June* 24, 1867.

" EXECUTIVE ORDER NO. 4.

" It is with deep regret that I have to announce to the people of this State the death at Burlington, Iowa, on the 19th inst., of Hon. Henry Dodge, one of Wisconsin's most honored public men.

" From an early day, General Dodge was actively and intimately connected with the affairs of Wisconsin, in the several capacities of Governor, Delegate in Congress, and United States Senator. At the close of his senatorial career, he retired from public life, and to the enjoyment of a dignified and happy seclusion, which he had so well earned by long and faithful service.

" A brave and accomplished soldier, an enlightened and incorruptible statesman—General Dodge was for many years recognized as one of the most distinguished leaders in the nation. Too brave to be other than he seemed, too honest to be a demagogue, his career was characterized by a manly independence in doing right, which won for him the confidence of the whole people.

"After a life, long and of rare usefulness, he has gone from our midst; and truly may it be said of him that to few indeed has it been given to leave a fame at once so wide-spread and so spotless.

"As a testimony of respect, the usual badge of mourning will be displayed at the several State Departments for the period of thirty days.

"LUCIUS FAIRCHILD,

"Governor of Wisconsin."

Many of these events are within the lives of this generation; but few, who have always lived in the advanced civilization of the metropolitan cities of the Atlantic coast, can appreciate the privations of the exile on the rude frontier, and the surpassing difficulties and hardships that must have been endured by the pioneers in achieving through sagacious and unremitting toil, with slow accession by emigration, their stupendous task of changing the savage wilderness into the grand State of beautiful Wisconsin.

In twelve laborious years this task was done, and its great career started in the Union. This work was conducted mainly by General Henry Dodge, around whom all naturally gathered as their leader in war and governor in peace.

Throughout his long career of fifty years of constant public service, in which he held with fidelity and distinction almost every public trust, civil and military, from his Western constituents, or by the President, to serve their interests; in steady and graded .advance, for his exemplary integrity and merit; at no time, even when his name was heard over the land for his wondrous skill and success in the Indian wars, did he swerve from his fixed habits of modest reserve and silence as to his own merits and services. He made no speeches, or sought popularity by the art of politicians, to build upon his fame such combinations as might give him National leadership.

This rare merit in our nation of selfish political orators, scheming for office and flooding the land with declamations of their own merits and claims, was in marked contrast with some of his contemporaries, who thereby secured their coveted reward of the Presidency.

Wisely. in modest self-sacrifice to his beloved constituents of Wisconsin, he chose the silent course of primary and unswerving fidelity to their interests, and calmly awaited the sober judgment of posterity.

Unquestionably the present grand results of his devoted life, are of far more enduring, and ever-growing public benefits to the North-west and to the Union, than all the forgotten party strifes and creeds of political aspirants that filled the air through the same period.

Such of these as are now remembered have been long since reversed; and almost all their fleeting policies are buried in oblivion, while the nation has outgrown their memory.

His immortal monument is his own grand State —Wisconsin.

The infant territory that he, as their chosen leader, began in 1836 to organize in all its life, from the frontier wilderness, and with such wisdom and integrity guided and controlled for twenty-one years, he had the satisfaction of witnessing its fulfillment of his hopes; to behold it rising into an imperial State, that sent over 200,000 of its sturdy youth to suppress the Southern Rebellion; blooming with fair cities, towns, and villages; with every culture and illimitable natural resources; with universities, galleries, and metropolitan elegance; traversed by steam on land and water; the proximate center of

population of the Union, and which since 1860 has
controlled the nation.

Augustus C., second son of Henry Dodge, was
born at St. Genevieve, January 2, 1812 ; reared in
the lead mines of Wisconsin, and denied the ad-
vantages of early education and training in the
schools and colleges now so abundant.

When but fifteen years of age, he served as a
private in several campaigns against the Winnebago Indians in a company of volunteers, commanded by Captain William Schuyler Hamilton,
third son of General Alexander Hamilton.

When twenty years of age he volunteered in the
Black Hawk War, and became a First Lieutenant
in the company commanded by Captain Francis
Gehoin.

June 18, 1838, he was appointed by President Van
Buren Register of the United States Land Office at
Burlington, Wisconsin, afterward Iowa Territory.

He discharged the duties of this office so accept-
ably to the people that, in 1840, they elected him
Delegate to Congress from Iowa, a position to
which he was chosen for four consecutive terms.

In 1848 he was chosen one of the Presidential
Electors of Iowa, and also United States Senator.

He drew into the two-year class, so called, and was re-elected for a full term of six years. He served in the two houses of Congress from 1840 to 1855. In the latter year he was appointed to succeed the Hon. Pierre Soulé as Envoy Extraordinary and Minister Plenipotentiary at the Court of Her Catholic Majesty.

For the manner in which he performed these important duties, we refer to the published letters of the late William Cullen Bryant, written from Madrid in 1859, page 150. He says:

" The American Minister, Mr. Dodge, is very attentive to the convenience of his countrymen, and a great favorite with such of them as come to Madrid. He is on excellent terms with the people of the country, and has done what, I think, few of his predecessors have taken the trouble to try, acquired their language. He has sent his resignation to Mr. Buchanan, that there may be no hesitation in giving the embassy to any other person; but, should the resignation be accepted, it is not likely that the post will be so well filled as it now is."

The eldest son, Henry Dodge, who had achieved distinction in the Indian wars under his father, and

had served as High Sheriff by election, and also as
Clerk of the United States District Court for Iowa
County, Wis., was appointed Agent for the Navajos,
whose language he spoke, as he also did that of
some ten other tribes; was captured by the Zuni
savages, and burnt to death at the stake. This
shocking act of savage barbarity was perpetrated
near Fort Defiance, New Mexico, in 1856. He left
a widow and four children, viz.:

George, late of Peoria, Ill.

Mary, wife of W. F. Fox, of Chicago.

Christiana, wife of Charles Rutter, New York.

Louis, New Orleans.

Israel Dodge, the grandfather, and his wife (Nancy
   Hunter), of Carlisle, Pa., settled at St. Genevieve, Mo.

   Children :

(Gen.) Henry Dodge.

Nancy, married (1st) James Conn, (2d) Rev. James
   Sefton.

Josiah (died without issue).

Israel, Jr., and his wife Louisa had six children
   (Arkansas).

John, wife and four children, all dead many years
   since.

Theodosia married Logan Caldwell, had six children; one only survives, viz., Henry L. Caldwell, of St. Genevieve.

Louis (died without issue).

Mrs. Rebecca W. Sire, of St. Louis, is now the only surviving child of Nancy.

The children of Israel, Jr., surviving are: George W., William H., Theodosia, and Mary, of St. Louis or Arkansas.

John settled in Arkansas, and his line is extinct.

General Henry Dodge married (1800) Christiana McDonald; had thirteen children, of whom nine, viz., seven daughters and two sons, grew to maturity.

Nancy married George W. Scott, brother of Hon. J. Scott, was Marshal of Arkansas, and died without children.

Louisiana, wife of W. J. Madden, Sonoma, Cal.

Henry (died 1856).

Augustus C., of Burlington, Iowa.

Elizabeth married Paschal Beguette, Vidalia, Cal.

Mary married John Dement, Dixon, Ill.

Selina married Myers F. Truett, San Francisco, Cal.

Christiana married Governor James Clark, Iowa.

Virginia married H. A. Hayden, Milwaukee, Wis.
Hon. Augustus C. Dodge and his wife Clara
(Herdich) have three children surviving, viz.:

Augustus,

Charles J.,

William, of Burlington, Iowa.

On the 20th day of November, 1883, in his
seventy-second year, the Hon. Augustus C. Dodge,
after a brief illness, died at his home in Burlington,
Iowa.

His death was deeply felt as of the most cherished
son of the State. From the very numerous obitu-
aries, the following is extracted:

CHANTING REQUIEMS.

The press of Iowa upon the death of General Dodge; re-
gardless of party they sorrowfully mourn a good and
pure man. A series of interesting sketches of and comments upon his life.

(From the Council Bluffs Globe.)

THE GREATEST ROMAN OF THEM ALL.

General Dodge was known to political life almost
from boyhood. His father was the late General
Henry Dodge, of Wisconsin, who was also an officer

of the United States Army, and the commander of
a regiment of dragoons in the Black Hawk War.
When Wisconsin was admitted as a State, the father
became one of its United States Senators, and the
illustrious son who has just died, was a resident of
the territory of Iowa, and its Delegate in Congress.
The latter served also in the Black Hawk War, under his father. As a Delegate in Congress, A. C.
Dodge exerted a powerful influence in securing the
admission of Iowa as a State, and when this was
accomplished, he was elected one of its Senators in
Congress together with General G. W. Jones, now
a resident of Dubuque. The most remarkable feat-
ure of this senatorial result was the fact that General Dodge, the father, of Wisconsin, and General
Dodge, the son, of Iowa, occupied seats in the
United States Senate at the same time; and both
took a decided and leading part in contemporaneous
legislation. It is due to the memory of the veteran
statesman who has just passed away, to say that
it is owing to his exertions, principally, that the
boundaries of Iowa were extended to the Missouri
River, so as to embrace the fairest and richest por-
tions of our great State. He was always devotedly
attached to the fame and fortunes of the Democratic Party, and when the control of Iowa passed

to the Republicans, General Dodge ceased to be its
Senator, but was, under the administration of President Pierce, sent as Minister to Spain, where he
won the esteem and confidence of all diplomatic
representatives of all the other Powers residing near
that court. Since his return from that mission he
has taken an active interest in political affairs. In
Congress he was an earnest and efficient advocate
of Pacific railways, and in all his senatorial career
enjoyed the peculiar confidence of Stephen A.
Douglas. General Dodge was a fine lawyer, and
during the last twenty years has devoted his remarkable talents to the practice of that profession.
In all his political and professional career General
A. C. Dodge has been characterized by the most
uncompromising and unswerving honesty. His
private character and reputation are untarnished.
He left official life, not richer as in these modern
days, but poorer by far than when he first entered
it. All classes of people throughout the State,
who knew this sterling character, will read the intelligence of his death with profound sorrow. He
was the greatest Roman of them all.

(*From the Davenport Democrat.*)

A HARDY, RESOLUTE, HONEST MAN.

The deceased was born at St. Genevieve, Mo., January 2, 1812, and consequently had reached the 72d year of his age. He was the son of Governor and General Henry Dodge, of Wisconsin. Nearly the entire life of the subject of this sketch was passed west of the Mississippi River, which is, of itself, a most exceptional fact. At the organization of the Wisconsin Territory in 1836, Henry Dodge was appointed Governor; what is now Iowa being included in that Territory, the capital of which was Belmont, for one year and afterward at Burlington. In 1838, Iowa Territory was organized and Augustus C. Dodge appointed by President Van Buren Register of the Land Office at Burlington. He is said to have made many friends among the early settlers by advancing them part of the money with which to pay claims. Soon after the time designated a dispute arose between Iowa and Missouri about the boundary line between them. General Dodge was one of the commissioners on the part of Iowa to settle the dispute, and afterwards he was commander of the Iowa forces when hostilities were threatened between the two commonwealths. It was

12

largely owing to his moderate course and concilia-
tory counsels that the matter was peaceably settled.

General Dodge served as a delegate for Iowa Territory in the 27th, 28th, and 29th Congresses. Upon
the organization of the State he was elected one of
the two first senators, and as such met his father,
who was also a member of that national body, having been chosen United States Senator from Wisconsin. General Dodge occupied his seat in the
Senate for eight years, taking a decided stand for
the interests of his State and constituents. He
served during the sessions of the 30th, 31st, 32d,
and 33d Congresses.

In 1855 he was appointed by President Pierce
Minister to Spain, and there continued during the
remainder of that President's administration and
also of President Buchanan's. In 1859, General
Dodge was the Democratic candidate for Governor
of Iowa, but he was defeated by Governor Kirkwood. He was a delegate to the Johnson Convention in Philadelphia and to the Chicago Democratic
Convention in 1864.

For several years following, General Dodge lived
as a quiet citizen in Burlington, of which city, in
1874, he was chosen as Mayor by a large majority

as a citizens' candidate. During the past summer the general took a great interest in the semi-centennial of Iowa's history, which was so successfully held at the city of his home. It may truthfully be recorded that the deceased was always a friend of young men, and was a favorite with them. Politically, he was always a Democrat, and temperance was one of the subjects to whose advancement he devoted much of his time and means. Many are the temperance organizations and red and blue ribbon clubs which trace their existence to his efforts.

It was in 1837 that he was married to Miss Herdich, of St. Genevieve, Mo., who survives him with the children, A. V., C. J., and W. W. Dodge, all residents of Burlington. In religion, the sympathies of the deceased were with the Catholic Church, of which Mrs. Dodge was a faithful member, and in the faith of which he was baptized during his last sickness.

In closing this hasty sketch, the materials of which have been hurriedly gathered, it should be stated that General Dodge was a strong partisan, and always engaged earnestly in the cause he believed to be right ; yet he commanded the highest respect of all, and was most esteemed by those who were brought into the most intimate relations with him.

His life will form a part of the State's history.
Whether he is viewed as a young man earning his
living by manual labor in the Galena lead mines, as
a flat-boatman on the Mississippi River, as Governor
of the Territory, or as a member of Congress, his
character stands out as a hardy, resolute, honorable
man, always devoted to his country, and doing the
important work assigned to him conscientiously and
well.

———

(*From the Burlington Hawkeye, November* 21.)

FEW MEN WITH CLEANER RECORDS.

General Augustus C. Dodge, Burlington's distinguished citizen, and one of the early pioneers of
Iowa, died at his residence in this city, No. 829
North Fifth Street, at 4 o'clock yesterday afternoon,
after an illness of only four days' duration.   The
intelligence of the demise of one who has been so
prominently identified with the history of Iowa, as
a State and a Territory, and whose life and public services have been so closely connected with the
history of this State—a man of generous impulses,
who never knew a selfish motive, kind, noble, urbane,
and charitable—will be received by the public with
profound regret and universal sorrow.

THE FATAL ILLNESS.

The first intelligence of the serious and fatal illness of General Dodge was made through the columns of the *Hawkeye* last Saturday morning. Thursday the General was upon the streets and apparently in good health. By undue exposure he contracted a severe cold and about 12 o'clock Thursday night he was taken ill and a physician summoned. His condition did not improve, and on Friday morning he was visited by Drs. Stone and Ransom. Friday evening he was resting quietly, but was under the influence of opiates administered by the physicians. At this time it was hoped by the numerous friends of the General that his strong constitution would enable him to completely recover, and his restoration to his usual good health was sincerely hoped for. Saturday he was in a critical condition, and in the afternoon an operation upon the bladder was successfully performed by Dr. Stone, assisted by Drs. Ransom, Nassau, and Henry. Temporary relief was afforded, but later in the night he suffered much pain. Sunday no encouraging symptoms had manifested themselves, and during the morning he grew worse and his condition became alarming in the extreme. A consultation of the medical advisers was held and another operation

was performed, which was followed by a chill. The
patient became delirious, his mind wandered, and
only at times did he recognize those about his bed-
side. Monday night he grew worse, and yesterday
morning he began failing rapidly and the physicians
gave up hope of recóvery. He continued to sink
through the day, and it was quite apparent that the
beloved man would linger but a few hours. At
3.30 in the afternoon there was a decided change
for the worse, for the hour of his dissolution had
come. A few minutes past 4 o'clock General A. C.
Dodge, surrounded by his sorrowing and aged wife,
his three sons, and one or two intimate friends,
quietly expired. The transition from life was
almost imperceptible. At the time of his demise
and for several hours previous the General lay un-
conscious. The death-bed scene was affecting beyond description of pen or tongue. Surrounded by
grieving relatives bowed down with sorrow, the
soul of that good and true man, General A. C.
Dodge, forsook its earthly tenement and winged its
flight to realms above.

The direct cause of General Dodge's death was
hermaturria of the bladder, the result of the con-
traction of a severe cold last Thursday. For the
past five years he has been afflicted with a chronic

disease of the bladder, the kidneys being also badly affected. General Dodge was a tall, stately, robust man, and possessed a splendid constitution, which repelled the attacks of disease until he reached a ripe old age.

General Augustus Cæsar Dodge was the son of Governor Henry Dodge, and was born at St. Gene-vieve, Missouri, January 2, 1812. When quite young he emigrated with his father to the lead mines of Wisconsin, coming up the Mississippi River in 1827, and locating at Galena, Illinois, long before the era of steam-boats. He won an honora-ble record in two Indian wars, the Winnebago War in 1827, and the Black Hawk War of 1832, distin-guished himself for bravery and winning deserved recognition for his services. He served as aide-de-camp to his father, Governor Henry Dodge, at the battle of Bad Axe, fought on the 2d of August, 1832, in Wisconsin ; where Black Hawk was defeated and his leaders captured in attempting flight to Canada. Shortly after the termination of this famous Indian war General Dodge was appointed Register of the Land Office which had been established at Burling-ton, and during his period of office formed an exten-sive acquaintance among the settlers upon the Black Hawk purchase, making numerous friends.

A sketch of General Dodge, published a number
of years ago, says that at the time he held this
office the " Club Law " was the tenure by which
every man held his land, and many a bitter, violent
quarrel originated between the settlers concerning
their respective " claims." Every neighborhood
had its own " Claim Association," where disputed
titles were settled and adjusted, but whenever
either party felt himself aggrieved by the decisions
of this " higher law court," an appeal was then
taken to the Land Office, where all the bitterness
and strife was again enacted. These disputes and
difficulties General Dodge settled in such a manner
as to give satisfaction to both parties, and made
him afterward the tried friend of either. No man
ever came to the Land Office, while he was in it,
but he went away showering blessings on the generous, noble-minded man who filled it.

The education of General Dodge in his earlier years
had been neglected, and it was during his term in the
Land Office in Burlington that he began to studi-
ously apply himself to self-education, from which
time to his death he has been an industrious student
and a constant reader. By constant application he
became a finished scholar and fitted himself for the
many public positions of trust he so worthily filled

subsequently.   General Dodge, in 1841, was elected
a Delegate to Congress from the Territory of Iowa,
and was re-elected for three consecutive terms, ter-
minating his career as a representative in Congress
in the year 1847.   He was selected as the presidential elector for the State of Iowa in 1848.   During
his career as a Delegate to Congress, he formed an
extended personal acquaintance among the leading
public men of the day.   The sketch of General
Dodge referred to above, says : " To see a man rise
from obscurity and poverty, untaught and unguided
by any other hand than his own, and rapidly force
his way through every grade of office almost ; with
credit and distinction, among senators and presi-
dents, kings, princes and emperors, courts and
camps ; is always a pleasing and interesting spectacle
to every true-hearted American, and sets to the
generation who are to follow him a bright and
glorious example."   No man ever worked with a
more fervent zeal for the benefit of a constituency
than he did, and no man ever procured for an infant
State or Territory what he procured for Iowa.   He
saw her future greatness, and by his unremitting and
indefatigable labor won for her, aid and assistance
that greatly accelerated her growth to its present
magnitude.   He knew what Iowa needed and pro-

cured it for her; his extended acquaintance and popularity enabling him to successfully consummate any project he undertook.

In 1846 was held the first Legislature after Iowa became a State, and the name of General A. C. Dodge was prominently mentioned for Senator, he receiving the unanimous support of his party. The contest between the Whig and Democratic Party for the election of members of the Legislature was a hot contest. The balance of power in the Legislature was held by three Democrats elected in Lee County, who were termed " opossums "; and had run independently of the political party of which they were members. These three Democrats refused to go into caucus and to support General Dodge; demanding that his name be withdrawn. General Dodge magnanimously offered to permit his name to be withdrawn, but his friends in the Legislature refused to consent to his proposition. Several attempts to elect him were fruitless, and the joint convention adjourned without making an election, and the consequence was that Iowa was without a senator for two years.

In 1848, the Legislature reconvened and he was elected United States Senator, with George W. Jones as his colleague, serving in the Senate until

1855. Among the measures aided and appropriations secured by General Dodge, were: An appropriation for a State road from Dubuque to the southern boundary line of Iowa; and an additional appropriation for completing State buildings; by personal intervention he secured the retention in office by President Tyler of the State Supreme Judges; he prevented the passage of an Act proposing to extend the limits of the half-breed tract in Lee County; procured a public land grant for improving the Des Moines River; procured a donation of 500,000 acres of public lands in Iowa for school purposes; and procured the removal of the Winnebagoes, a band of Indians that was constantly committing depredations. He also during his congressional career aided in procuring an appropriation of $100,000 for clearing out the obstructions in the rapids of the Mississippi, and an additional appropriation of $125,000 for the construction of snag dredge-boats for Western rivers, and procured the passage of a bill granting lands for railroad purposes in Iowa. He opposed the "Bennet Land Bill," and defended the "Union and Compromise;" advocated the passage of a "Homestead Exemption" law, for the protection of the poor class; opposed monopolies and labored in behalf of any measure he thought would improve the condition of the laboring class. He played an important part in the early national legislation, and was the contemporary of Webster, Clay, Calhoun, Silas Wright, and Senator Phelps. General Dodge sat in the Senate with his father, and this is the only instance of a father and son holding seats in the Senate at the same time.

General Dodge received the appointment of Minister to Spain from President Pierce, and the nomination was unanimously confirmed. His amiability of character, his experience in the halls of the national legislature, his untiring energy, innate talent and ability well fitted him for a diplomat. His nomination at the time was generally favorably commented upon by the press of the country, although James Gordon Bennett, of the New York *Herald*, opposed the appointment through the columns of his paper, and heaped abuse upon General Dodge, which was entirely unwarranted by existing circumstances. At the time of the appointment, the Washington *Union* commented as follows upon it :

" The unanimous confirmation of the distinguished Senator from Iowa for the position of American Minister to Spain, shows how highly the Senate of the United States appreciated the wisdom of the selection by the President. General Dodge is a genuine type of the American character. His has been a most interesting career. He has, as it were, grown up with the mighty West. Still a young man, his history is crowded with eventful details. He has been tried and proved in every emergency, and from his first hour in public life down to the present moment, he has been regarded as a man of eminent capacity and lofty integrity. His frank and fearless character, his sagacity and experience, will make him a worthy representative of his country. One thing is certain, the President could have taken no man who more faithfully reflected the patriotic sympathies of the National Democracy, or who has been more completely identified with that sentiment of political action which regards the Constitution and the Union as one and inseparable."

During General Dodge's eight years' residence at the Court of Madrid, he discharged the duties of Minister with promptness and in a business-like manner. Mr. and Mrs. Dodge were favorites in society and of Queen Isabella; the latter one day presenting Mrs. Dodge with a handsome oil painting of herself on copper plate, and of her husband, which are now at the residence of General Dodge.

General Dodge finally resigned, and returned to Burlington. In 1859, General Dodge ran for Governor on the Democratic ticket against Samuel J. Kirkwood, but was defeated. The nomination for Governor was forced upon him, as he declined it. Immediately following his defeat, he received an unsolicited complimentary vote for United States Senator from the Democratic members of the State Legislature, fifty-two in all, which was tendered as a mark of their undiminished confidence in General Dodge. His defeat in the race for the gubernatorial chair was in reality General Dodge's political downfall. But he did not pass into obscurity, and would not, no matter how long he might have lived.

General Dodge was a delegate to the Chicago Convention of 1864, and also to the Philadelphia National Convention of 1866. In 1871, while the nominees for the approaching presidential campaign were being discussed, the name of General Dodge for President on the Democratic ticket was mentioned in a number of newspapers, and he was freely spoken of among his friends. His name was also mentioned for the Vice-Presidency. General Dodge presided as Chairman of the State Democratic Convention, held at Council Bluffs, at the opening of which he made a stirring speech, and was a delegate

to the Capital Convention held at St. Louis a number of years ago.   He participated in all presidential and State campaigns, and made numberless
political addresses.   On an Eastern tour in 1879, he
was frequently mentioned by the leading journals of
that section of the country, and met many of the
friends he had made while engaged in public life.
General Dodge also wrote a lecture entitled, " Spain
and the Spaniards," which he prepared some ten
years after his return from that country as Minister
Plenipotentiary.   It was delivered in a large number
of cities and towns.   General Dodge has attended
numberless old settlers' reunions in Iowa and Illinois,
and the limitless fund of incidents and reminiscences
of early pioneer life which he possessed always
made him an interesting and entertaining talker at
gatherings of this character.   He was elected Mayor
in 1874, and has assisted in various projects for the
improvement of the city.   About the latest matter
that engrossed his attention, and in which he acted
a prominent part, was the semi-centennial celebration held in this city on the 1st of June last.   General Dodge was made Chairman of the Executive
and Invitation Committees, and was the presiding
officer of the day, and to his untiring efforts and
advice was much of the success of the celebration

due. On that day he delivered an able address,
replete with historical reminiscences, and met hun-
dreds of his old-time friends. Since the celebration
he prepared and had printed a pamphlet containing
a record of the commemoration of the fiftieth anni-
versary of the settlement of Iowa; the distribution
of which among his friends he had about completed.

HIS CHARACTER.

General Dodge was a man with a spotless reputation, and during a public career of fifty years not
one breath of suspicion has been uttered against
his name. He was generous to a fault. No one in
need of assistance ever came to his door without
receiving aid. He was noted for his urbanity, and
no one was so humble that he would not stop upon
the street, speak to and shake hands with. His
sympathies were instantly aroused for the op-
pressed. He was kind-hearted, magnanimous,
pleasant, and agreeable. In appearance he was
stately and dignified. He possessed a high order
of ability, and discharged his public duties with
a devotion and earnestness worthy of imitation by
modern statesmen. He was a man of accurate
judgment, and possessed a large capacity for labor.
He was honorable and upright in every transaction,

and leaves a spotless record that will forever perpetuate his name in the history of Iowa.   He was a strong advocate of temperance and every measure for the alleviation of the poor classes.   He belonged to no religious denomination during his life-time, but attended church regularly.   Several days previous to his dissolution he was baptized in the Catholic faith.   To him home was a sacred shrine; there he found the greatest joy and contentment. He was an affectionate husband and a kind father. His family relations were always agreeable.   He was a man of strict integrity, and charitable to the last degree, and was a good neighbor.   Few men leave behind them the clean record General Dodge has. He was known to every person in Burlington, and his death will cause deep public sorrow.

To Mrs. Dodge, who is an aged lady, and the General's son, the sympathy of the entire community is extended.   Countless friends called at the residence of the General yesterday evening to extend their condolence and offer such assistance as might be in their power to render.

General Dodge leaves three sons, A. V. Dodge, and C. J. and W. W. Dodge.   The former is engaged in commercial pursuits, and the latter are attorneys, having built up a splendid practice.   The

13

General had seven sisters, four of whom are dead. They were: Mrs. Nancy Kingsbury, Mrs. Elizabeth Beguette, Mrs. Governor C. H. Clark, Mrs. Virginia Hayden, Mrs. L. Madden, now residing in California; Mrs. Mary L. Dement, mother of Henry Dement, Secretary of State of Illinois, of Dixon, Ill.; and Mrs. S. Truett, of San Francisco. He had one brother, Henry Dodge, who is dead. General Dodge had one daughter, who died some thirty-five years ago.

General Dodge left a will bequeathing all his property to his wife. It is to be regretted that he has not left a history of his life, as it has been an eventful one. It is remarkable that no biography of General Dodge could be found in any of the State, county, or city publications, and the one presented this morning is prepared from the memory of old citizens and a scrap-book which contains many newspaper articles referring to the General. It may be possible there are a few errors, but in the main it is correct. Some one should undertake to write an extended biography of the General.

BLOCK ISLAND

AND ITS HISTORY.

To the wearied brain-toilers of the cities, courts, or pulpits, and the scheming merchants ever weaving new plans of stupendous effort for gain in new ventures; to each and all come seasons when the overwrought mind, nerves, and muscles must have repose to insure future activity.

A large class whose taste, or perhaps lack of reflective taste, are best pleased with the gilded lounging, and the idle, flirting, affected, and pretentious butterfly throng of the vast summer caravanserai hotels.

But, for those who seek delicious climate in a home on the rolling, solemn sea; with every desired luxury from garden, field, and waves, in bracing air; an elixir of new heaven-born life and serene quiet; where, undisturbed, one can ride, walk, bathe, fish, and sail in ever-renewed variety, or study the grand features of its local history, and learn how it became such a nursery of heroes and freedom—above all other summer resorts is Block Island.

Consult any good map, and the beautiful island, deep rooted in the ocean bed, will be seen lying due south of the main shore of the central part of Rhode Island, thirteen miles away; about eighteen miles north of east from Montauk Point, and twelve miles from the north shore of Long Island; circled round by the open sea, a mass of *treeless*, fertile hills and pastures, affording in every direction views of the wide Atlantic, far as the eye can reach, always crossed by the ever-moving steamers and white-winged sailers of the seas.

Rev. Samuel Niles, in his rambling narrative (A. D. 1700) of the Indian wars, describes Block Island during his own residence there (1674–1762). After detailing the completion of his large stone house there by Captain James Sands, adds: " In 1689 the island was captured by French privateers, and on his advice, Mr. Niles, Mr. Sands and family, with some others, ' took our flight into the woods, which were at considerable distance, where we encamped that night. After which the three elder brothers, Captain John Sands, Mr. James and Samuel Sands, removed to Long Island and settled there, each leaving a farm at Block Island, which they stocked with sheep, and came over once a year, at shearing time, on Block Island, to carry off their wool and fit sheep for market at New York.' "

According to the coast survey, its position is in latitude 41° 08' north, longitude 71° 33' west. It is about eight miles long, of irregular shape, and about three miles wide.

> " Circled by waters that never freeze,
>   Beaten by billows, and swept by breeze,
>   Lieth this Island of Manissees."

The visitor arrives at its harbor and breakwater, to stay the surging Atlantic (the recent Government work), just south of the old harbor and Clay Head, and not far above the commanding South Light, in full view of Beacon Hill, the church, and pleasant homes of the islanders ; and as he walks the cliffs will have broad ocean views of ever varying life.

The visitor may find many days of invigorating exercise, rambling in this fine air and scenery, over the island, its shores and waters ; but he will, perhaps, seek his leading interest in the study of its history in its unique ancient records, with the excellent Town Clerk, Ambrose M. Rose, Esq.

We record gratefully our obligation to this venerable contemporaneous Record—almost unexampled in this country—for some of the original material of the following historical sketch of the island, its discovery, title, and settlement.

For the massive breakwater, new harbor, the beautiful and commanding South Light-house, as

well as for the grand "Ocean View Hotel," whose
palatial proportions first greet the visitor, the island
and the public are indebted to the well-directed
energy and public spirit of the Hon. Nicholas Ball.
He is a native. His ancestor, Hon. Peter Ball, arriving
on the island from England early in the eighteenth
century, was prominent in the General Assembly of
the Colony of Rhode Island, and in 1735 obtained
the first pier for the island. His present representative, whose maternal ancestor and wife are of the
family of the original settler—Tristram Dodge—has
become, by his true beneficence and large-hearted,
sagacious, and untiring enterprise, justly the foremost citizen of Block Island. Besides these prominent works, to him is also due the life-saving station
and the submarine cable to the main-land.

He has for eighteen years—from 1854-72—con-
tinuously, and often by unanimous choice, repre-
sented the island in the Assembly and Senate of
Rhode Island. No history or description of the
island would be complete without this imperfect
tribute.

Block Island, from its discovery, in 1614, by
Adrian Block and Hendrick Christiansee; where
they built a fort and a few houses (sailing in their
yacht—length 64½ feet, breadth 11½ feet—the

"Onrust," or Restless, the first vessel built at New Amsterdam, through Hurl Gate and the Sound to Boston, and discovering Long Island to be an island) remained in possession of its native Narragansett Indians, who called it " Manissees," which is alleged to mean " Little God." Block Island was named on Dutch maps after this voyage "Adrian's Eylandt" and " Block's Eylandt." A skipper from Massachusetts, Captain Oldham, and his crew, having been massacred by the Indians, whose repute was generally peaceful, and Oldham doubtless provoked the assault, Endicott and Underhill, with their force of one hundred men, landed and severely punished the Indians; whereby Massachusetts Bay claimed title to the island, to which the Indians yielded and paid tribute.

In the year 1658, Massachusetts Colony granted it to Endicott, Bellingham, and associates, but no settlement ensued.

In 1660, John Alcock, M.D, of Roxbury, apprized, so runs the record, Thomas Terry, James Sands, and other associates in his land schemes, that he knew of an adjacent island that could be bought for £400, and that if they would divide this sum and all expenses they might share the profits, on condition of paying him twenty-five acres or £5 for one-sixteenth. His proposal being accepted, they took an assignment of the title of Endicott and his associates, and at a meeting at Alcock's house, September, 1660, appointed Peter Noyes and Thomas Faxun (called " knowing men ") as survey-ors, to lay out the island in lots for the settlers: of whom sixteen engaged and paid all expenses of building, jointly, a barque at Braintree, and equip-ping the same ; which, however, made too slow progress for Simon Ray and Samuel Dering, who built a " shallop " at their own cost. In April, 1661, the " shallop," navigated by William Edwards and Samuel Staples, sailed from Braintree to Taun-ton, and there received its fifteen settlers and their families. Thomas Faxun having proceeded with the surveyors previously.

What a rare sight now would be that old " barque," so heavy and slow ! and that " shallop," so swift and sure !

We might compare the " barque " with the " Mayflower " in size and capacity ; and marvel at the number of the Plymouth Pilgrims, with the crew, freight, etc., that we are annually trumpet-called to hear from the modest New Englanders.

Without the least parade of exile, covenant, or form of government for Church or State, the set-

tler owners of the island, of ample resources, quietly
sailed away from New England's arrogant exclusive-
ness, to establish in their favored island, a truly free
State and Church, which never sought to impose
restrictions on others.

In the very ancient parchment-bound Town Records of New Shoreham, or Block Island, familiarly
called " The Old Sheepskins " and legally the " Evidences of Property," appears the following record:

" Memorandum in the year of our Lord 1660, as
followeth:

Mr. John Alcock, physician in the town of Roxbury in the colony of Massachusetts, being connected with Mr. Thomas Faxun, Peter George,
Thomas Terry, Richard Ellis, Thomas Dering,
Simon Ray, all of Braintree, with sundry persons
belonging to other towns.

Mr. John Alcock, acquainting them of an island
that was to be sold, namely, *Block Island*, which
might make a situation for about sixteen families;
and also declaring the price to be four hundred
pounds; and that, if they would be concerned with
him proportionally towards the creating a plantation on Block Island, he the aforesaid John Alcock
would then proceed in the purchase thereof; granting him for his trouble and pains, five pounds for a

sixteenth part or twenty-five acres of land as an equivalent, and to be at equal proportional payment for said purchase in manner and form as followeth:

Twenty-five pounds for every sixteenth part; the remainder of the payment for to be paid in coun-try pay, such as the country afforded; and accord-ingly timely notice was given unto all those that might think convenient for to be concerned with the erecting the concerns aforesaid, for to make their personal appearance at the house of Mr. John Alcock, August the seventeenth, 1660; then and there accordingly was forthwith attended by those hereunto subscribed,

Mr. John Alcock, M.D.,	Simon Ray,
Thomas Faxun,	Felix Wharton,
Peter George,	Hew Williams,
Thomas Terry,	John Gluffer,
Richard Ellis,	Edward Vorse,
Samuel Dering,	John Rathbone,

and according to the aforementioned premises forthwith agreed with Mr. John Alcock for the pay-ment of said island proportionably as above men-tioned; and also a consultation for which way to proceed concerning the erecting a plantation on the aforesaid Block Island, considering the remoteness

thereof both by land and sea, and could not be settled without great charge ; whereupon some of our
company began for to decline ; still the remainder
proceeded in the management thereof as noted ; all
and every person that was concerned with land on
Block Island should be at their equal proportion
of all charges belonging unto the settlement thereof.   Whereupon for the premising and settlement
of Block Island it was agreed upon that whose
name here subscribed Mr. James Alcock, Felix
Wharton, Hew Williams, Thomas Terry, Samuel
Dering, Simon Ray, all of them agreeing forthwith
to build a barque for the transporting of cattle
to said island for the settlement thereof.   Thomas
Terry, Samuel Dering, Simon Ray, procuring the
hull for to be built ; Mr. John Alcock, Felix Wharton, and Hew Williams for to provide the sails, and
riggings, and accordingly proceeded in the management thereof.   Further, for the better and quicker
transporting of passengers, considering that there
was no harbour, Samuel Dering and Simon Ray
built a shallop upon their own cost and charge for
the promoting and settling of said island, and by the
end of the year 1660 the barque and shallop were
finished for the same purpose before mentioned,
and William Rose, first master of the barque for

the employment that the barque was built for, and
William Edwards and Samuel Staples undertaking
to sail the shallop around the Cape, and for to meet
the passengers at Taunton, there to take them
in and sail for Block Island. In the year 1661 the
barque set sail for Braintree. In the beginning of
April, for Block Island. The shallop received its
passengers at Taunton, namely:

Thomas Terry,	Duncan Williamson,
Samuel Dering,	John Rathbone,
Simon Ray,	Edward Vorse,
William Tosh,	Nicholas White,
Thormutt Rose,	William Billings,
William Barker,	Trustarum Dodge,
David Kimball,	John Ackus,
William Cahoone,	(Thomas Faxun had pro-
	ceeded with the surveyor).

"Memorandum in the year of our Lord 1661.
Further settlement of the Plantation of Block
Island.

"Notice was given unto all the proprietors to
assemble themselves at the house of Felix Wharton, in Boston, the first Tuesday in September,
1661, there to consult and agree upon some able

and knowing man to survey the island, that every
purchaser might have his proportion, that he or
they might improve it to the best advantage they
could; Mr. John Alcock propounding unto the assembly thereof, a man that he knew for to be an
able proved surveyor, one Mr. (Peter) Noyes, of Sud-
bury; forthwith the assembly accepted Mr. Alcock's
proposal, and forthwith it was voted that Mr. Noyes,
Mr. Faxun, an able knowing man, that they should
go to Block Island and by lot divide unto every
man concerned his due proportion as near as they
could; and so accordingly they did proceed in the
managing thereof according unto direction of the
purchasers and proprietors of said island that took
it into consideration at the time of this assembly,
and agreed upon, that there should a quantity or
portion of land be laid out for the help and main-
tenance of a minister, and so continue forever, and
accordingly Block Island was surveyed and lotted
out proportionally unto the ·purchasers by Mr.
Noyes and by Mr. Faxun, as doth appear by the
surveyor's works in the plot and draught of said
island, measured and bounded unto every purchaser
according to proportion by lot as followeth:

"The North part of the island by lot:

"Mr. Richard Billings, lot 1.

" Samuel Dering, lot 2.

" Nathaniel Wingley, Turmot Rose, lot 3.

" Edward E. Morse, John Rathbone, lot 4.

" Thomas Faxun, lots 5 and 6.

" Richard Ellis, lot 7.

" Felix Wharton, lot 8.

" John Glover, lot 9.

" Thomas Terry, lots 10 and 11.

" James Sands, lot 12.

" Hew Williams, lot 13.

" John Alcock, lot 14.

" Minister's land, lot 15.

" Peter George, lot 16.

" Simon Ray, lot 17.

" Western part of the island as by lot divided:

" Thomas Faxun, lots 1 and 2.

" Nathaniel Wingley and Turmot Rose, lot 3.

" Thomas Terry, lots 4 and 5.

" Felix Wharton, lot 6.

" John Alcock, Physician, lot 7.

" George S. Ray, lots 8 and 9.

" South-east part of the island:

" John Rathbone and Edward, lot 10.

" Richard Billings, lot 11.

" Richard Ellis, lot 12.

" Hew Williams, lot 13.

" John Glover and James Sands, lots 14 and 15.

" Samuel Dering, lot 16.

" The other small divisions by lot divided unto every purchaser by proportion.

" The above written on both sides being a true copy abstracted out of the old Book of Records of Memorandum for the first settling of Block Island by me.

" November 29, 1695,

" Pr. Nathaniel Mott,

"Town Recorder."

Upon this title did these settlers embark all their means and lives; no other title was obtained either of Indians or Dutch, whose cession by treaty with England in 1664 came opportunely. These early settlers and proprietors of Block Island, unlike all other American colonists, sought no royal charter or authority from Europe, as their basis of title; and they took possession of their purchase and remained in quiet enjoyment for three years of their respective lands; undisputed sovereigns; until the negotiation of Roger Williams induced their formal and voluntary adhesion to his new colony. The specu lators sold out at profit to the settlers who had no other deed than the survey and map of 1660; only one copy whereof, and very imperfect, is now extant on the island, and with Mr. Simon Ray Sands, copied for his grandmother.

The sixteen settlers entered into possession of their allotments; and here have ever since remained undisturbed by the natives, or the several wars of the colonies and States. When, in 1664, Rhode Island was chartered by Charles II., they elected to become part, and not of Massachusetts; and those settlers, by Delegates James Sands and Joseph Kent took the oaths as Freemen of Rhode Island, as appears hereby:

Rhode Island Colonial Records, 1664–77.

(Prov. 1857), printed by order of the General Assembly, vol. xxi., p. 58. "At a General Assembly of the Collony of Rhode Island and Providence Plantation, assembled Rhode Island, the fourth of the third month (" May ") so-called, 1664, and in the sixteenth yeare of the raygne of Charles the Second, King of England, Scotland, France, and Ireland, etc.

" Whereas (recital that it hath pleased the King to grant a charter to the colony), wherein Block Island is expressly nominated as part of this colony.

"That by these messengers: James Sands, Thomas Terry, and Joseph Kent, the inhabitants of Block Island have declared unto this Assembly their professed obedience to his Majesty said royal pleasure.

(After settling form of government, oaths of allegiance and office to be subscribed and filed), proceeds: ·

" Whereas Mr. James Sands, of Block Island, being freeman in this Collony or Corporation of Rhode Island and Providence Plantations, etc., together with Joseph Kent, of Block Island, hath presented their humble petition to this Court, being the Generall Assembly of this Collony, in behalf of Thomas Terry, Peter George, Simon Raye, William Harris, Samuel Dearing, John Raurbone, John Davies, Samuel Staple, Hugh Williams, Robert Gutney, William Tosh, Tallman Rose, William Carhouse, *Tristrome Dodge*, John Clark, Joseph Kent, and William Barker ; inhabitants and housekeepers at Block Island aforementioned, desiring that the forementioned inhabitants may be admitted freemen of this Collony aforesayed, and being demanded, if they the said James Sands and Joseph Kent did know that all the forenamed persones weare men of peaceable and good behaviour, and lykly to prove

14

worthy and hopefull members of the Collony, they
answered 'Yea,' where upon the Court on caution
and instructions given to the sayd petitioners, have
accepted and admitted all the sayd inhabitants
aforementioned, to be free of the sayd Collony, or
soe many as shall give under their hands in writting
according to the instructions aforementioned."

It is not a little strange to remark the *providential
preservation* of this island; alike from the Puritan
intolerance of Massachusetts; the monarchical ambi-
tion of conquest of the French, its first discoverers,
under Verazzano, so zealous to plant the lilies and
the Church in the new world, on his discovery,
naming it Luisa, for the king's mother, when, in
1524, he described it to Francis I. accurately in geography, "and as full of hills covered with trees, well
peopled, for we saw fires all along the coast ":— ·

And also, from the energy of the Dutch West
India Company, that claimed title to all Long
Island, and vigorously attacked the Cow Bay settlers; as well as from any sympathy with dynastic
changes in England, or much activity in our own
Revolution ; yet the island commands Long Island
and its Sound, as well as Narragansett Bay.

Its first settlers were Baptists, and the *only*

church building and society on the island is of the Baptists, and so has been from the beginning of its history.

This first church was organized (October 3, 1772) by Thomas Dodge, Hannah Dodge, and six others (eight in all), Thomas Dodge, Deacon. The first pastor was Rev. David Sprague; second pastor, Rev. Thomas Dodge ; Deacons, Oliver and Tristram Dodge. This church constituted itself, and adopted its own Articles of Faith.

It was created and still flourishes in the true spirit of independence and freedom of religious conviction, after the model of Roger Williams.

From early in the last century the island has been treeless, and yet very fertile, with its fine manure of sea-weed and peat, and now there is only one young orchard here, and tree planting has scarcely begun.

The settlement of Block Island, in 1661, is of much interest to the reflective student of the well-springs of our national and family history. It must have been by reason of the general ignorance of geography that, although the colonists of Massachusetts Bay were active sailors and traders with the colonies of Connecticut, New Haven, and Hartford, and the Dutch of New Amsterdam ; although Mas-

sachusetts, in 1636, through the organized raid of
Endicott and Underhill, and their little army, had,
according to the existing theory, obtained and
asserted political sovereignty over the island as part
of its soil; yet the island, with its advantageous position and resources, was wholly unknown and unexplored beyond the landing-place of their expedition;
and although the Dutch Admiral Block, with Commander Hendrick Christiansee, had, in 1614, sailed
around the island, landed, explored, fully described,
discovered, and took it into possession for Holland,
erecting a fort and some dwellings thereon in the
same voyage in which he fully discovered Long
Island; sailing around it and fixing its geographical
position, prominent points, and coast-line;—upon
which voyage of first discovery, the Dutch had uni-
formly asserted paramount title and sovereignty to
all Long Island, very efficiently by their West India
Company of 1624, whose Directors-General were
vested with full civil and military powers as Governors of the New Netherlands at New Amsterdam,
on the Island of Manhattan;—neverthless, the island
remained unoccupied by any Europeans before 1661.
It is not a little strange, when, over a century previous, the adventurous Frobisher and Raleigh had
penetrated, the one to the regions of the Arctic

Circle, and the other to Virginia, in the "South Sea," following the lead of Cabot; when constant trade was maintained to the East Indies and the Carribbean Islands; and no distance deterred the equally adventurous Hollanders, who were already planted in Java and South America; and were keen in their search around the globe, over whose sea they claimed and exercised supreme dominion, for advantageous colonial settlement; that this lofty and fertile island, in constant sight from the main-land, as well as from Long Island, and commanding, by its position at the entrance of the Sound, its whole commerce, as well of Long Island as the main shore; should have been suffered by the Dutch to lapse from their sway, and their original title of discovery and possession be yielded to oblivion; and that the English skippers, on their frequent voyages along the Sound, and enterprising English emigrants had never ventured to its shores; and at such a late period, this near neighbor to the colonies was almost wholly unknown and only occupied by its aboriginal Indians. The plain solution is that *it was providentially reserved* for a settlement unex-ampled in all history; for a *pure democracy* and *entire religious and civil freedom*, its leading charac-teristic to the present day.

This grows more marked as we study the history of the great maritime nations of that age. In the fifteenth and sixteenth centuries, Spain was the unquestioned Mistress of the Seas; and, from the era of Columbus, Pizarro, and Cortes, with Portugal and Holland, had founded vast empires in Asia, Africa, and America; Holland early became their successful rival, and then England and France emulated their search for new lands and productive colonies.

This spirit of maritime adventure, so conspicuous in England during the reign of Elizabeth; became under her Stuart successors, more generally organized and constant; and, as with the Huguenots of France, was the chosen refuge from oppression, attracting their best spirits. The second generation of Massachusetts colonists only followed herein the policy of their ancestors; by emigrating to new soil from the intolerant bigotry of the authorities at Plymouth, Boston, and Salem, and their equally restricted Colony of Connecticut.

Massachusetts Bay Colony, in 1658, by patent granted the island absolutely as their private property, free of all claims of sovereignty, to John Endicott, Richard Bellingham, Daniel Dennison, and William Hawthorne. Their title of absolute

fee simple was, in 1661, acquired through Dr. John
Alcock, of Roxbury, Massachusetts, by the sixteen
original settlers in like full estate, as their own absolute private property, of which they became and
continued undisputed sovereign proprietors.

The island was not insignificant and therefore
unvisited. Of about the area of Manhattan, with
fertile soil and abounding in the harvest of the seas;
its first settlers, like the "Lotos Eaters," would go
home no more; they remained and reared their
families in content, and their descendants still own
and occupy the island. Save for this providential
reserve, some of the striving European colonizing
nations would have covered its hills with fortifica-
tions like Malta, Rhodes, or Gibraltar; or, in America,
Quebec or Louisburg, to become a sanguinary bat-
tle-ground.

The first settlers of 1661, with their families,
numbered thirty, and the Indians were estimated
at four hundred, of peaceful, industrious habits.
In 1700, the whites had increased to two hundred,
and the Indians declined to three hundred and fifty
in number, and steadily failing. In 1800, there were
only sixteen Indians to seven hundred and fourteen
whites, and from 1860–76 only *one Indian*—last of
the Warrior Narragansetts—is returned with eleven

hundred and forty-seven whites; and that solitary representative has since disappeared.

It appears elsewhere of record that the above petition of Sands and Kent had been referred to, and reported favorably by, a committee, of which Roger Williams was Chairman; and doubtless the same master spirit induced their mission and negotiations with the islanders.

In 1672, it was incorporated as the Town of New Shoreham (from the ancient town in Sussex, on the coast nine miles west of Brighton), otherwise Block Island, and its officers, elected 1676, were:

Peter George, Head Warden or Justice Supervisor.
Simon Ray, Deputy   "   "
James Sands, Adjutant "   "
Robert Guthreg, Town Clerk.
Turmot Rose.
William Tosh, Constable.
Tristram Dodge, Sen. Sergeant.

And this Act of Incorporaton is substantially in force to this day.

From the recent official list of voters in New Shoreham, R. I., entitled "A list of all persons that possess property to the amount of one hundred and thirty-four dollars and over, who will be qualified to

vote in all legal organized town meetings on all
questions in said town, under article second, section first of the Constitution."

The total of such qualified voters is 183 ; of whom
the " Dodges " named are 34, the most numerous of
all the families there ; succeeded by the " Little-
fields," with 33 names.

At the ordinary ratio of one-sixth, the above
would assume a resident population of at least 204
Dodges; at the date of this poll, or over one-sixth
of the total population of the island.

From the beginning—now over two hundred and
twenty years ; the settlers steadily increasing, have
by their marine enterprise visited every navigable
sea in their staunch, double-ender schooners; with
large inland and foreign trade, through their fisher-
ies ; and yet no village has ever existed there ; no
foreigners have ever joined their community ; which
is unexampled for unity of religious faith and political convictions.

The contented islanders awaited till 1832, or 162
years, before they had a local post-office ; and 220
years, or till 1880, before the first daily mail came by
a steamer.

Although well educated, by their excellent public
and other schools long established, and the busy

islanders have long visited all seas; yet, never has
there been a newspaper or magazine printed there;
telegraph, railroad, lawyer, or physician settled on
the island.

They are content, busy like the Hollanders, and
too thrifty to waste their brief time in looking after
the affairs of others.

They show many of the distinctive traits of Holland; in their sturdy battle with the sea in its rage
—so fierce upon their bleak shores; as well as the
proverbial Dutch constancy, frugality, and, untiring
industry; with the simplicity, honesty, frankness,
and genial tolerant hospitality of the rural natives
of Northern Vermont.

The islanders by their position are a distinct, un-
mixed race; of sterling virtues; which their descendants should be proud to emulate.

COW NECK, LONG ISLAND.

SINCE 1860, purposelessly disguised, in the pretentious name of Port Washington, a sea-port—not
of entry—without docks, village, or hotel—or even
definite bounds; the little settlement has but scant
interest to the driving crowd of traders from all
lands that throng the metropolis with their weary

strife for the dollar, and like Bunyan's Muckworm, are ever bent downwards raking over their little compost-heap ; and will not pause to look up to the long vista of history about this pleasant neighbor, nor learn its golden lessons.

Some, however, may be interested by family ties, old associations, or antiquarian taste ; and for such these pages are offered.

Cow Neck and Cow Bay are upon the north shore of Long Island, about thirty-five miles east of the city of New York, and about one hundred and thirty miles by the usual course west of Block Island.

Cow Bay, about one mile wide and a half mile in depth, extends on the west from the point of Great Neck ; due south of which and on the bay lies Manhasset, or "Little Cow Bay," as formerly called ; and on the east, from Sands Point on the Sound along Plum Beach, Dodge Island, Dodge Pond and Mill Dam to the main shore.

Cow Neck is the elevated land around Cow Bay on the west, and Hempstead Harbor on the east ; including Sands Point on the Sound ; Plum Beach, Dodge Island and Pond, Cornell's mill, dam, and residence, and the ancient estates of Thomas Dodge, and Petrus Onderdonk: comprising all the land from the hills to the shore on both sides of Hempstead Harbor, and originally contained 6,000 acres.

Since 1784, on the division, it is in the township of North Hempstead.

Sands Point derives its name from the purchase, December 25, 1691 : and deed to John Sands (son of Captain James Sands of Block Island) from Richard Cornell, of Rockaway, and his wife of 500 acres of land at Cow Bay, L. I., which included this point. Cornell held under a grant from Governor Dongan in 1686.

Mr. Sands resided there till his death in 1712 : in his house still standing: which remained in his family till about 1765, when it passed to Benjamin Hewlett with the existing family burial-lot.

By the successful discovery, voyage, and landing, claiming for the House of Orange in 1614; of Adrian Block and Hendrick Christiansee, which was followed by their settlement at " Breukland " Amersfort (New Town), New Utrecht, Gowanus, etc., on the western extremity, and scattered settlements on the north shore: Long Island was rightfully Dutch territory, and the Dutch claims were vigorously asserted.

But in 1635 Charles I., for value, and probably in contented ignorance of its actual situation, extent or importance; and of the existing Dutch possession by valid title; by patent granted all Long Island to Alexander Earl of Stirling and Devon, who, through his agent James Fassett, became the source of title subsequently to many farms and lands on the eastern end.

In 1640 these titles came into conflict according to Governor Winthrop in his Journal, April 4, 1640.

"The inhabitants of Lynn finding themselves straitened, looked out for a new plantation, and going to Long Island they agreed with Lord Stirling's agent, one Mr. Fassett, for a parcel of land near the West End and with the Indians for their right. The Dutch, hearing of this, and making claim to that part of the island by a former purchase of the Indians, sent over to take the place, and set up the arms of the Prince of Orange upon a Tree," and gives a copy of the original agreement with Fassett and several of Lynn, dated April 17, 1640, and of a deed from the Indians, dated December 13, 1640.

Thompson's History of Long Island, vol. i. p. 40, gives a more detailed narrative.

"A few English emigrants from Lynn, having

contracted with the agent of Lord Stirling for a parcel of land upon Long Island, undertook a plantation on the west side of Cow Neck, and near the head of Cow Bay, afterwards called Howe's Bay; from Lieutenant Daniel Howe, Conductor of the expedition, and sometimes Schout's Bay, from such officer being sent to arrest settlers. Dutch Governor directed Secretary van Tienhoven, with the Under Sheriff and twenty-eight men, to go to the Bay, and meet the intruders; they brought six men to Nieuw Amsterdam, who being examined, confessed that they came from Lynn under direction of Mr. Fassett, agent of Lord Stirling."

These settlers, of whom no list is preserved, were not baffled, but allowed to remain, doubtless by acknowledging the paramount authority of the Dutch; as an additional muniment of title: and thereby were expressly included, and reaped the benefit of the treaty of settlement and amity between the Governor of the New Netherlands and the Indians of Long Island, signed by six Sachems, dated 12th March, 1656, which is expressed to extend to and include all the English as well as the Dutch people within their jurisdiction and to the Dutch lines.

(Hempstead Town Records, Book A, page 40.)

But in 1643, Hempstead alleged that she made a purchase of all their lands from the Indians, though no deed is extant or pretended.

And so, in 1656, Hempstead puts on record (in her own books, by her clerk):—

Ib. p. 43, well written in English, a Confirmation "by the Indians of Mansapage, Mericoke, and Rockaway, and all the rest of yᵉ Indians that doe claim any rights or interests in the purchase that Hamsteede bought in the year 1643, and wᶜʰ is in the boundes and limits of the waste Tract of Land concluded upon with the Governor of Manhattans, as it is in this paper specified" (with formal covenants of confirmation and for quiet enjoyment).

Signed by several Sachems, and by their "tokens" or emblems.

Next follows on the old Hempstead Records (p. 45), in the ("English") receipt of the Indian Sachems; the "Generall Boundes of the Lands that Hempstead claimed to have bought of the Indians in 1643, viz.: "Beginning at a place called Mattagaretts Bay; and soe running up on a direct line North and South, from North to South; and from sea to sea, to the Boundes, running from Hemsteede harboure, due Easte, to a poynte of trees, adjoining to the lands of Robert Williams, where we left marked trees, the same line running from sea to sea. The other line beginning at a marked tree standing at the East ende of the greate plaine, and from that tree running upon a due South line, and at the South Sea by a marked Tree made in a neck called Mackactchoung, and from thence upon the same line to the South Sea."

Within above spacious, — free and easy, — "Boundes" of the wilderness, — by its sons — Hempstead always claimed to include, and exercised jurisdiction over the region of Cow Neck.

Certainly—if Hempstead ever bought of the Indians—it were impossible to refute their claim on these "Boundes":—evidently of their own preparation.

The Sachems, with ponderous titles and emblems, disappear; and the Town Sages of "Hemsteede" feeling securely intrenched by these wordy and windy documents, so solemnly recorded at full length, proceeded to set apart the undefined region of Cow Neck; as the Common of pasture for the Town; where the cows, sheep, etc., of its residents could roam throughout the season; having been duly marked by their respective owners, and these marks, being recorded annually in the Town Records; whereby they were to be safely returned to winter quarters. These marks are frequently and fully recorded; and probably this is among the earliest examples of the introduction here of the ancient English local custom of common of pasturage.

This was, of course, the origin of and established the name of the region as *Cow Neck* or *Cow-pasture Neck*.

Of the Hempstead Records, it is appropriate to say that the extant Records from Book A begin with 1657 and seem continuous. A book of the Records from 1644–57 is lost. This is called the lost "worm-eaten" book.

It is hard to refrain the thought, that if really Hempstead had any valid Indian title in 1643, its own Records would surely have set it out at length; and the *only* missing volume could not have contained it, or it would have been as carefully preserved as its successors. No copy of the entries in this volume is extant.

Is it unjust to those so long past away, after our experience of their ability in making wild Indians speak to their purpose; that they thought it most

15

prudent to put out of sight their own record—and entries coeval; that would defeat all pretence of valid Indian title in 1643 ?

Much stranger things occur daily and happened then.

Besides the solemn records of the marks upon the pasturing herds on Cow Neck, and frequent repetition of the name incidentally as a locality, the first specific entries I find in these Records are in Book B, page 52 : " Firman Haring is to burn the Cow Neck this year 1665; and is to have 12 shillings in good pay for his payens."

April 1, 1681, page 101.

" At a towne held at Hemsted there was Lett to Danill Beadel the Cow Neck called ye Raybridg for   £01.00.01."

" Hemsteed, April the 23d, 1669 " (p. 179), " at a General Town Meeting, and by major vote, it is ordered and agreed upon, that all those that have fence at the Cow Neck shall have right in the Neck according to the fence which he makes for pasture land, and if ever hereafter the Cow Neck shall be lotted into particular allotments, then every man shall have a proportion, according to the fence that he maketh, and none to have right but only those who have fence theare ; and further it is ordered, that no man shall put any more cattle there than they have made fence."

The affairs of Cow Neck and Hempstead pass unrecorded, and doubtless in tranquillity, until the Town Meeting of the 15th of December, 1683, when "John Codman, Jackson, and Searing, are chosen to go to New York, to agree with *Mr. West* concerning their land- at Cow Neck, to try for *an arbitration;* if not, the town will pay the money and proceed according to law."

This entry, brief and abrupt, seems the first knowledge that the solemn Supervisors had of this valid and paramount title of John West.

John West, who in 1676 was settled in New York City, married Anne, daughter of Attorney-General Thomas Rudyard; who, from his services as Governor of East Jersey, became Attorney-General of the Province of New York, and served as such 1684 and 1685, when he was appointed Governor of Barbadoes.

John West, in 1680, was Secretary of the Ducal Province of New York. In 1661, he had obtained a grant of this land from the Dutch Governor (No. 538).

This patentee had held the indisputable paramount title of all their lands at Cow Neck during
all this period, in which they had been busy getting
up their records.

No further mention hereof appears; doubtless
they found it most convenient to submit rather
than "proceed according to law"; and that discretion was the better part of valor against a patentee
of such potent connections, and official rank; and
they agreed upon a suitable compromise.

Much coveted Cow Neck and all the "Hemsteed"
lands were covered by another patent, making the
third sovereign grant of all their undefined Indian
mythical title.

On the 16th of November, 1644, his "High
Mightiness" William Kiefft, Governor and Director-
General of the Nieuw Netherlands, by direction of
his employers, exercised the original, rightful, and
supreme authority over Long Island, of the States
of Holland, by issuing his Patent of that date to
Robert Fordham and six other Englishmen (one of
whom had been employed to build the church in
the fort at Nieuw Amsterdam), and unto their heirs
and successors, or any they should join in association with them, "for all the land, with all the havens,
harbors, rivers, creeks, woodlands, marshes, and all

other appurtenances thereunto belonging, upon and
about a certain place called the Great Plains, on
Long Island, from the East River to the South
Sea, and from a certain harbor known by the name
of Hempsted Bay, and westward as far as Matthew "
(Martin) " Garretson's Bay ; to begin at the head
of the said two bays, and to run in direct lines, that
they may be the same latitude in breadth on the
south side as on the north, and as far eastward ";
but with a condition, " in case the patentees and
their associates shall procure one hundred families
to settle down within the limits of five years after
the date hereof ; and if the patentees cannot within
five years procure one hundred families to settle on
said lands, they shall enjoy, ratum pro rata, land
according to the number they shall procure ; giving
full authority to build a town or towns, with fortifi-
cations, and erect a temple or temples to use and
exercise the Reformed Religion, which they profess,
with the ecclesiastical discipline thereto belonging ;
and with full power and authority to erect a body
politic, or civil combination among themselves, and
to nominate Magistrates, to be presented to the
Governor for choice and appointment, &c., &c.
Reserving as rent the tenth part of all revenue that
shall arise from the ground manured (or cultivated)

with the plow or hoe—gardens and orchards not exceeding one Holland acre excepted."

This liberal grant of a principality, with independent government and church and perpetual dominion, embraced the present limits of Hempstead and North Hempstead, extending across Long Island, north to south at its widest, and in breadth east and west about eight and one-half miles.

The towns of Jamaica and Flushing, afterwards patented in like terms by Governor Kiefft—the latter in 1645—are on the west, embracing now a part of the land originally granted to Hempstead.

In 1647, under this patent, allotments of land at and about Hempstead were made to sixty-six proprietors, whose names and antecedents are elaborately stated in the careful "Early History of Hempstead," by Charles B. Moore, Esq.

None of these allotments appear to have been made on Cow Neck, which still remained, although under new masters, common of pasture, and only began to be separately granted by the town from about 1670.

Thomas Dodge, of Block Island, born in 1684, grandson of Tristram Dodge, one of its sixteen original settlers of 1661, settled at Cow Neck, and

doubtless erected the antique homestead on Dodge
Pond, where his descendants still live. There he
died, 1755. His lands appear on the Map of actual Survey of all the lands on Cow Neck (L. I.)
"by I. G. Clowes, Surveyor, dated 1695," now at
the homestead, by the name of "West's Patent,"
and run from the present western line of the lands
of William Miles, deceased, to the mill of Cornell.

Thomas Dodge, the original settler of the name,
had not yet come at the date of Clowes' map. He
was settled there pursuant to his deed of January
11, 1719, to Tristram Dodge, his brother, shortly
before that date. The conveyance to Thomas
Dodge is not of record at Hempstead, but by his
deed to his cousin, Samuel Dodge, of Hempstead,
dated " 5 George I. and the year of man's salvation
1718," of a farme att Hempstead of fifty-nine acres
"and twenty-six square rods, or one-third lacking
five acres of that farm that was Samuel Clowes,
bounded eastwardly partly by Thomas Dodge aforesaid, and partly by Tristram Dodge, and westerdly
by Rigbell Mott ; westerly by other lands laid out
upon gate right, and northerdly by the land belonging to the heirs of John Carle, deceased ": it is
plain that, prior to 1718, Thomas and his brother
Tristram Dodge were settled on Cow Neck, and that

Thomas acquired land at an earlier date (perhaps about 1710) from Samuel Clowes.

By the ancient records of New Shoreham, R. I. (Block Island), copied in 1695 by Nathaniel Mott, Town Clerk, it appears, viz. :

" Thomas Daudge, son of Thrustarum Daudge, born January 23 of January, 1684."

" Samuell Daudge, son of William Dodge, Sen., born September 19, 1691."

These grandsons of the first settler were first cousins; their fathers being brothers.

By the time of his legal majority, or twenty-one years, Thomas may be presumed to have acquired land there, viz.: from about 1705–10, and his cousin Samuel from about 1712–20.

From these have descended many very numerous and well-known branches of the family in the city and State of New York; whose generations have, like their ancestors, planted new lands at the West and risen to much social and official eminence; presenting a good record in the Colonial and Revolutionary Wars, besides that of 1812, and the late Rebellion.

The Dodges settled at Cow Neck after the Motts and Clowes; but they can show an unbroken possession of near two hundred years in their ancient house, that has tranquilly looked upon the convulsive struggles of this long period; an extraordinary example of constancy in ancient foot-prints: during centuries that have witnessed the ceaseless movement of nations into new lands, and their transformation in laws, customs, and manners.

Adjacent to their land, between it and the ancient Manor of Onderdonk, is the old cemetery, called after the name of the Onderdonk Manor—the Flower Hill Cemetery: on its beautiful and commanding hill, overlooking the Bay and main shore.

The ground had been immemorially a burial-place; but in 1786, by deed of Daniel and Aertje Rapelye to Adrian, Peter, and Hendrick Onderdonk, Martin Schenck, Ann Rapelye, Thomas Dodge, Andrew Hegeman, Sen. and Jr., and Albert Hegeman, Sen. and Jr., and their heirs; Flower Hill was expressly conveyed by due bounds to the above families, for their use as a family burial-place forever.

Here, in ranks—separated—lie the generations of the dead. Andrew, son of Thomas Dodge, who died 1762 at 28 years, is the eldest. There are in all fifteen grave-stones of the Dodges, down to Richard of 1873.